Primitive Baptism
...and Therein Infant's and Parent's Rights
by Matthew Sylvester
with chapters by C. Matthew McMahon

Copyright Information

Primitive Baptism and Therein Infant's and Parent's Rights
by Matthew Sylvester, with chapters by C. Matthew McMahon
Edited by Therese B. McMahon

Copyright ©2019 by Puritan Publications and A Puritan's Mind®

Some language and grammar has been updated from any original manuscripts. Any change in wording or punctuation has not changed the intent or meaning of the original author(s) and has been made to aid the modern reader.

Published by Puritan Publications
A Ministry of A Puritan's Mind® in Crossville, TN.
www.apuritansmind.com
www.puritanpublications.com

All rights reserved. No part of this publication may be reproduced, stored in a retrieval system or transmitted in any form by any means, electronic, mechanical, photocopy, recording or otherwise, without the prior permission of the publisher, except as provided by USA copyright law.

This Print Edition, 2019
Electronic Edition, 2019

Manufactured in the United States of America

ISBN: 978-1-62663-343-8
eISBN: 978-1-62663-342-1

Table of Contents

Meet Matthew Sylvester 4
To the Reader 8
Preface 10
CHAPTER 1: Primitive Baptism 11
CHAPTER 2: Objections Answered 27
CHAPTER 3: Two Resolutions 37
Appendix 47
Appendix 2 49
Other Helpful Books by Puritan Publications 99

Meet Matthew Sylvester
Edited by C. Matthew McMahon, Ph.D., Th.D.

Matthew Sylvester (1636–1708) was a nonconformist divine, son of Robert Sylvester, who was a dry goods merchant. He was born at Southwell, Nottinghamshire, about 1636. From Southwell grammar school, on May 4, 1654, at the age of seventeen, he was admitted at St. John's College, Cambridge. He was too poor to stay very long at college, but as he kept up his studies while supporting himself in various places, probably by teaching, he became a good linguist and well-read in philosophy.

In 1659 he obtained the vicarage of Great Gonerby, Lincolnshire. He was a distant relative of Robert Sanderson (1587–1663), who became bishop of Lincoln in 1660. In the wake of the *Act of Uniformity* he resigned his living in 1662, rejecting Sanderson's offer of further placement. He now became domestic chaplain to Sir John Bright, and subsequently to John White, a Nottinghamshire Presbyterian. In 1667 he was living at Mansfield with Joseph Truman, but in that year he came to London, and became pastor of a congregation at Rutland House, Charterhouse Yard. He was on good terms with many of the London clergy, particularly Benjamin Whichcote and John Tillotson. Richard Baxter, who remained to the last in communion with the church of England, and declined to be pastor of any separated congregation, nevertheless became, from 1687, Sylvester's unpaid "assistant." He valued Sylvester for his meekness, temper, sound principles, and great pastoral ability.

Baxter's eloquence as a preacher supplied what was lacking to Sylvester, whose delivery was not as powerful as Baxter, though in prayer he had a remarkable gift, as Rev. Oliver Heywood notes. After Baxter's death in 1691 the congregation declined. Early in 1692 it was removed to a building in Meeting House Court, Knightrider Street. Edmund Calamy, D.D., (who was also Sylvester's assistant from 1692 to 1695), describes him as "a very meek spirited, silent, and inactive man," in straitened circumstances. After Calamy left him he plodded on by himself until his death. He died suddenly on Sunday evening, January 25, 1708. Calamy preached his funeral sermon on February 1st.

Sylvester's Works:

He published four sermons in the "Morning Exercise" (1676–90); three single sermons (1697–1707), including funeral sermons for Grace Cox and Sarah Petit, and "The Christian's Race...described [in sermons]," 1702–8, 8vo, 2 vols. (the second edited by J. Bates). He wrote *prefaces* to works by Baxter, Manton, Timothy, Manlove, and others. His chief claim to remembrance is as the literary executor of Baxter. In 1696 he issued the long-expected folio, "Reliquiæ Baxterianæ. Or, Mr. Richard Baxter's Narrative of the most Memorable Passages of his Life and Times;" appended is Sylvester's funeral sermon for Baxter. No book of its importance was ever worse edited. Sylvester, an unmethodical man, had to deal with "a great quantity of loose papers," needing to be sorted. He insisted on transcribing the whole himself, though it took his "weak hand" above an hour to write "an octavo page."[1] During the progress of the work he was "chary of it in the last degree" (as Calamy notes), and with great difficulty brought to consent to the few excisions which Calamy deemed necessary. In addition to a fatal lack of arrangement, the folio abounds in misprints, as Sylvester "could not attend the press and prevent the errors." The "contents" and index are by Calamy, who subsequently issued an octavo "Abridgment" (1702, 1714), much handier but very inferior in interest to the "Reliquiæ."

For Further Study:

---

[1] Preface, §1.

Reliquiæ Baxterianæ, 1696, iii. 96; *Funeral Sermon* by Calamy, 1708; Calamy's *Account*, 1714, pp. 449 sq.; Calamy's *Own Life*, 1830, i. 312, 359, 376, ii. 80; *Protestant Dissenter's Mag.* 1799, p. 391; Wilson's *Dissenting Churches of London*, 1808, ii. 105; Hunter's *Life of O. Heywood*, 1842, p. 193; Mayor's *Admissions to St. John's Coll. Cambridge*, 1882, i. 115.

To the Reader[1]

The author of these papers is one whom I have known for a long time to be a person of great reputation for knowledge, wisdom, gravity and seriousness. He is a person not only skillful and diligent in his particular calling, and beautiful in his Christian conversation, but also a diligent and judicious reader and observer of the sacred scriptures; and, this I learned of others, or myself discerned by conversation with him being an impartial searcher after the truth, and readily receptive of it in its discerned evidence. And, consequently, he was not tenacious of any sentiments or opinions through humor, interest, and self-conceitedness where any reasons do appear to prove them false, or probably uncertain or unsafe.

That this small tract is his, I have great reason to believe. It is small and clear as to its great design; of which, the title is a sufficient indication and account of its contents. Let the matter speak for itself, and force its way into the readers breast by its own strength, carried home by God's blessing on this to such degrees as he sees

---

[1] This work was originally titled, *Primitive Baptism, and Therein Infant's and Parent's Rights*, based on Matthew 19:6, "What God hath joined together, let no man put asunder." Published in London, Printed for Jonathan Robinson, at the Golden-lion in at St. Paul's church-yard, 1690.

fit, who is the original Source and Fountain, Patron, and End of truth.

I shall only add, that when our brethren who judge it improbable that any infants had their solemn admission into the church of Christ in scriptural times by the instituted rite of Christian baptism, have tried their strength on what is here offered, and scripturally proved, and have effectually answered what is here briefly, and in other books, more copiously demonstrated and improved, they may probably gain more proselytes to themselves. Read carefully, think deeply, pray fervently, design honestly, judge impartially, and give Christ's evident truths, laws, and institutions, their just receptions and improvement; and take in nothing for truth or duty for the sake of any man, but yield to evidence; and this will be most grateful.

Preface

As a person's *civil right* is one of the great controversial points in the world, so is religious right in the church.

What is here offered concerning infant's and parent's right in the church, is a short discourse maintained against two different practices; the one withholding baptism from infants of baptized parents; the other withholding such parents from their infants in baptism.

The arguments brought against these practices, are those brought by Christ against a practice of the same nature, namely that it is a *putting asunder those whom God has joined together*, and *that from the beginning it was not so.*

These arguments are not insisted on as suspecting the strength of other arguments, but as agreeing with them, and better to clear up the apostolic practice in these things.

And all these are submitted to superior judgements.

To yours in and for our Blessed Lord,
MATTHEW SYLVESTER.

CHAPTER 1:
Primitive Baptism

God "who at sundry times, and in diverse manners, spake in times past unto the fathers by the prophets, hath in these last days spoken to us by his Son." This Son (that our religion and manners, faith and worship, may follow after *his* due order) has commanded us "to search the scriptures," containing rules and directions, precepts and examples, always evident and perfect in their kind, though not always in the same way expressed.

The Sadducees finding no express mention of the resurrection in the books of Moses, (which they emphatically called *the scriptures*) not only denied the resurrection but framed an argument from those scriptures against it. One of these arguments they thought was so unanswerable (Deuteronomy 25:6), that they encountered Christ himself with it (Matthew 22:23-24, *etc.*). Christ observing their confidence, reproves them as plainly both of error, and the cause of this, in these words, "ye do err, not knowing the scriptures, nor the power of God" (verse 29); and from the scriptures proves the resurrection.

These words of Christ, "Ye do err, not knowing the scriptures, or the power of God," may have a double aspect, one to the scripture, from where they framed their argument against the resurrection, and another *to the scripture*, which he brings to prove the resurrection by.

That the Sadducees did not know the scriptures literally, or the power of God historically, cannot be the meaning of Christ; but take the words as having an eye to that scripture brought by them (verse 24) from where they raised their argument against the resurrection, and the sense may be such *as this:*

> You Sadducees say that there is no resurrection, and you seem very confident of your opinion, as if you were in the right, and had scripture on your side, and could from the scripture prove it to be impossible. But I tell you, "Ye err, not knowing the scriptures, nor the power of God"; for though that is scripture which you have quoted, yet you, not comparing it with other passages of the same sacred writing, nor scriptural writings, nor spiritual things with spiritual, do not hold the analogy of faith contained in the scriptures. Instead, you speak evil of those things which you do not know, while what you know naturally as brute beasts, in those things, you corrupt yourselves. For the dead are raised is even proven by Moses who showed this at the burning bush when he called the Lord *the God of Abraham, and the God of Isaac, and the God of Jacob, for he is not the God*

of the dead, but of the Living, for all live to him. And though you pretend to know God, yet you do not glorify him as God, nor consider that power belongs to him. Otherwise, why should it be thought as an incredible thing to you, that God himself should raise the dead? Neither are your notions of the future state, to which the dead are raised by his infinite and almighty power, suitable to those high and excellent apprehensions which you ought to have of it. For, in the resurrection they neither marry, or are given in marriage, neither do they die anymore, but are as the angels of God in heaven. *You therefore do greatly err.*

But taking the words of Christ as having a respect to the scripture by which he brings to prove the resurrection (verse 32), then the meaning may be as follows, or something like this:

> You deny that there is any resurrection, and conclude that you must be right, because you find no express mention of it in the scriptures, and as if the incapacity of the dead made it impossible with God. But you are wrong in this, because you do not know the scriptures, nor the power of God. For though it is not expressly said that "the dead are raised," yet know that there is

sufficient proof for it in Scripture by good and warrantable inference from Scripture. For concerning the resurrection of the dead, have you not read that which was spoken to you by God, saying, "I am the God of Abraham, and the God of Isaac, and the God of Jacob?" (Matthew 22:31). From there you might have attained the knowledge of the resurrection as *satisfying*, as if it had been expressly said, that the dead are raised. For, God is not a God of the dead, but of the living. If you had considered this, you might have known that the spirits of men, though separate from their bodies, are there by the power of God, (the God of the spirits of all flesh) still held in life. You would know that God can and will by the same power, according to his working, able to subdue all things to himself, raise their bodies, and unite to them their spirits. These inferences, being agreeable to the holy scriptures, and a true and right asserting of the power of God, are *as scripture*, of which you are willingly or wilfully ignorant, and have erred in this main article of religion.

Now though the Sadducees still persisted after such conviction in their error, saying that "there is no resurrection," and in opposition to the doctrine of Christ (Luke 20:37, 38) that "there is neither angel nor spirit," yet the way of *proving* by *consequences* is not less cogent or commendable.

And if the resurrection might be in this way proved, then, why not other points? Why not the baptizing of infants in the same way following Christ's method of interpretation?

It is true, the resurrection is not worship, yet it is an article of faith, which if it is not believed, all our worship is in vain. And though nothing is to be admitted into the worship of God, as such, which is contrary to the expressed precept and command by consequences, yet these rightly drawn from scripture, are no less a rule for our practice, than they are for our faith (1 Corinthians 15:13-14, *etc.*).

Now the baptizing of infants has been abundantly proved from time to time by many plain and undeniable *consequences*. It is rightly inferred from scripture, and in this manner in which Christ proves the resurrection, applying that to infant baptism *should satisfy us*. Yet, since the expressed precept or example are so much called for, let us inquire into this a little to understand it.

Christ's first commission about baptizing is not recorded, but must be gathered from his second commission, and from the practice of the disciples, and acts of the apostles.

The second commission of Christ for baptizing, is Matthew 28:19, "Go ye therefore, and teach all nations, baptizing them in the name of the Father, and of the Son, and of the Holy Ghost, *etc.*"

The practice of the disciples and apostles were to baptize particular persons, and with parents, their house and household; as Lydia and all her household (Acts 16:14-15), the jailor and all his household (verse 33), and Crispus and all his house (Acts 18:8).

Question. The question is, whether these were only adults, or adults *and* infants?

Answer. They were adult and infants. These words, "household, his, and house," when spoken of people, being a Hebraism for "children of the house," who are the seed of the house (1 Samuel 2:33; Deuteronomy 25:5; Matthew 5:12, 19), whether they are infants or adult children.

In this way Genesis 34:30 says, "I and my house"; and 41:13, 19, "Pharaoh said, take your father, and your little ones, and your wives, and come;" and Genesis 46:31, "My brethren, and my father's house are come." Numbers 16:32, "And the earth opened her mouth, and swallowed them up, and their houses," that is, their sons and little children (verse 27) in other words, of Dathan and Abiram (Deuteronomy 11:6), whereas of Korah it was all the men that appertained to him, as in the same 32nd verse, not his house, for in 26:11 it is said that the children of Korah "died not." Judges 9:16, "Now therefore if ye have done truly—and dealt well with Jerubbaal and his house: (for my father fought for you, *etc.* And ye are risen up against my father's house, and have slain his sons) if ye have dealt truly and sincerely with Jerubbaal and his house, then rejoice, *etc.*" 1 Samuel 3:12-14, "In that day I will perform against Eli all which I have spoken concerning his house, *etc.*" 2 Samuel 3:1, 6, "Now there was long war betwixt the house of Saul, and the house of David, *etc.,*" and chapter 7:16, 18, 19, 23, 29, "Thine house shall be established, *etc.*" And chapter 9:3, "And the King said, Is there not yet any of the House of Saul?" and chapter 12:10, "Now the sword shall not depart from thy house." 1 Kings 13:34, "And this thing became sin to the house of Jeroboam." 1 Chronicles 13:14, "The Lord blessed the house of Obed Edom;" (that is, chapter 26:4-6, "his children"), and chapter 1:16, 43, "David returned to bless his house." Psalm 114:1, "When Israel went out of Egypt, the house of Jacob from a people of a strange language." Micah 2:2, They oppress "a man and his house." Habakkuk 2:10, "thou hast consulted shame to thy house." Luke 19:9, "This day is salvation come to this house." Titus 1:11, "Who subvert whole houses."

Add to these Genesis 7:1, "And the Lord said unto Noah, come thou and all thy house." So, chapter 18:19, "I know Abraham, that he will command his children, and household after him" (that is, his children who are his household after him; for no others of the family, though it did not exclude them, were properly his household after him, but his children, called his seed after him). In this way see chapter 30:30, "And now when shall I (says Jacob) provide for mine own house also?" So Exodus 12:27, "It is the sacrifice of the Lord's Passover, who passed over the houses of the children of Israel, when he smote the Egyptian, and delivered our houses." Thus Deuteronomy 25:9, "So shall it be done unto the man that will not build up his brother's house." So 1 Timothy 3:4-5, "One that rules well his own house, having his children in subjection with all gravity: for if a man know not how to rule his own house, how shall he take care of the Church of God?" And chapter 5:8, "But if any provide not for his own, and especially for those of his own house," which according to the same apostle, 2 Corinthians 12:14, is his children, "For the children ought not to lay up for the parents, but the parents for the children."

In this way we see the Hebraism of these words; "household," "his" and "house" in scripture, according to which these words in these three first cited examples of Lydia, the jailor and Crispus, are by some very great interpreters rendered, "the children of the house;" and are necessarily to be so taken there, infants not being excepted, unless some sufficient reason can be given to the contrary.

Now the main reason to the contrary given, is, that these "houses" and "households" who are said to be baptized, were such as to whom the words of the Lord is said to be spoken, and who are said to believe in the

Lord, which it is pretended they could not do if spoken of infants; so that there were either no infants there, or no infants there baptized.

But this reason is not sufficient, because it supposes these "houses" and "households" to be said to have the word of the Lord spoken to them without the parents, and so renders infants incapable; where, take "house" and "household" with "parents" and "infants" have been, and so may be, of them to whom the word of the Lord has been spoken. In this way children were of those to whom Moses made that great and solemn exhortation Deuteronomy 29:2, 9-11, "And Moses called unto all Israel, and said unto them ... Keep therefore the word of this covenant ... To stand all of you before the Lord your God; ... your little ones, your wives, ... that ye should enter into covenant with the Lord thy God, and into his oath, which the Lord thy God maketh with thee this day." And of them to whom Joshua made that famous repetition of the law, Joshua 8:34-35, "And afterwards he read all the words of the law, the blessings and cursings according to all that is written in the book of the law. There was not a word of all that Moses commanded, which Joshua read not before all the congregation of Israel with the women and the little ones."

And though it is said in Nehemiah 8:2-3, "Men and women, and all that could hear with understanding," yet it is not said them only, as if infants were excepted, neither does it follow that they were; for we know that whatsoever the law says, it says to them that are under the law (Romans 3:19). And we are sure, that the command of Moses, Deuteronomy 31:11-13, was, that the solemnity there appointed, should be with the women and the children. Also, this applies when he called to all Israel, in Deuteronomy 29 as mentioned before, and made that exhortation, "they stood before him with their little ones, and their wives." Likewise, when Joshua made that rehearsal of the law in Joshua 8, "It was before the whole congregation, with the women and little ones." So, 2 Chronicles 20:13, "And all Israel stood before the Lord with their little ones, their wives and their children." Still women with their little ones and children, as if such little ones, as by reason of their infancy did yet hang on the tender breast. Agreeable to that is Joel 2:12, "Turn ye unto me ... with weeping and mourning: (verse 13), rent your hearts, ... (verse 15) call a solemn assembly ... (verse 16) gather the people: sanctify the congregation: assemble the elders: gather the children, and those that suck the breast, *etc.*"

Not that parents ought therefore to bring their little ones at all times to the reading and preaching of the word; but this shows that it was done on some great and solemn occasions, when they entered into *covenant* with God, or the like. And "little ones" may be part of those to whom the word of the Lord is spoken (Acts 21:5).

It is granted, the phrase and manner of speaking in scripture is primarily accommodated to those who are *adult*, but not exclusively of infants; for they, as Israelites, were of those to whom, the apostle says, "appertaineth the giving of the law," (Romans 3:19). And, as Jews, "of them to whom were committed the oracles of God," (Romans 3:1-2; Acts 7:38).

Secondly, this supposes these "houses" and "households" to be said to believe without the parents, and so though it had instead of "house" and "household," been said "their children, little ones, and babes;" yet according to this supposition and assumption the meaning would have been made *still the same;* that this could not be of such those who are in age, but only of such in quality and disposition. Where, take it as it is, "parents" and "house" together, and then "infants" are not only included, but *chiefly intended,* the adult being for the most part at their own disposal, while the infants were always at the disposal of their parents. They themselves, whether heathens or Jews, being converted to the faith of Christ, brought over theirs, all if possible, but *be sure* they brought their infants, to be of the same faith with themselves. And it being *parent* and *house,* and *not house without the parents,* who are said to believe, this shows it to be *in a way of covenant,* which *always* includes the infants. And this as the infants of heathens were always reputed to be heathens, and the infants of Jews to be Jews, so the infants of Christians to be Christians, (Matthew 18:6; Galatians 6:10; Ephesians 2:19) (though not declaratively so, no more than the converted adult until baptized). And this may as infants of such, as well be said to believe, as the infants of circumcised parents might be said (by being circumcised) to become debtors to do the whole law (Galatians 5:2). Or, by not being circumcised, *to break the covenant* (Genesis 17:14).

Objection. But it is said, "Faith comes by hearing," (Romans 10:17). How then can infants be said to believe?

Answer. This goes on the former mistake of putting "parents" and "infants" as separate ideas or classes, for so it is said, "He that believeth not, shall be damned," (Mark 16:16), "and is condemned already," (John 3:18). Shall not infants therefore be saved? God forbid, for though they cannot believe in all respects as the adult does, yet they may be parties with their parents in the covenanting part of their parents' faith, as their parents covenant for themselves *and them*; which is very well illustrated by parents making their infants parties with them in their own civil contracts of bonds and leases, but is grounded only on the nature of the covenant of God. As this faith comes to the parents by hearing, so it comes to their infants in conjunction with them.

When therefore it is said *such and such*, as namely, the jailor, Crispus, and the nobleman, John 4:53, "believed with all their house," this related not so much to the great success the gospel had in those times, though that was very great, as it relates *to the covenant of God with parents and their children*; because no house is said to believe without the parents, nor any parents without the house under their charge without the house itself; which must therefore have a respect to infants, adult people sometimes believing, and not their parents; and parents, and not always the adult.

A husband might believe and not the wife; the wife, and not the husband. But though it is said to a husband or a wife, "Believe, and thou shalt be saved, and thy house," yet it is not said to any husband, "Believe, and thou shalt be saved, and thy wife;" or to any wife, "Believe, and thou shalt be saved, and thy husband;" but only, "What knowest thou O wife, whether thou shalt save thy husband? Or, how knowest thou, O man, whether thou shalt save thy wife?" (1 Corinthians 7:16).

Again, a master might be converted, and not the servant; a servant might be called, and not the master; but with considerable difference *in respect to the house*. When the master being a parent, believed, there salvation came to *the house*, but this is not so when only the servant of a house was called, or believed. This is one reason which the apostle gives there, why a brother or sister being married, should not depart from, put away, or leave their unbelieving yoke-fellow (verse 10-14). This is why the converted servant should not leave his unconverted master (verse 20-23).

And this makes clearer that *the house* in the scripture must include infants, in that a house is said to be saved, (that is to say, saved as to the outward means of salvation; which to them who die in their infancy may be to their eternal salvation); where the parents are said to be saved, but not the house said to be saved without the parents. In this way when Peter was sent to Cornelius (Acts 11) it was to tell him words by which he, and all his house should be saved. The same which Paul and Silas here said to the Jailor (Acts 16). And so every parent, "believe in the Lord Jesus Christ, and thou shalt be saved, and thy house," which must be with respect to infants. For, as it would be hard to say that infants could not be of the house which was to be saved; so it would have been needless to say, *the house was it, not for the infant's sake.* The adult of every house, if they believed being saved, whether the parents believed or not; so the it would also make the excluded infants from being *of the house*, and it makes all those grants of salvation made to the house on the *parents* believing; such as that to Zacchaeus, Luke 19:9, "This day salvation is come to this house, forasmuch as he also is a son of Abraham." And here to the jailor, "Believe in the Lord Jesus Christ, and thou shalt be saved, and thy house," to be superfluous, and insignificant. For, the adult of every house, as said before, were saved, if they did believe, though the parents did not believe, nor were saved; *but no house is said to be saved without the parents.*

Question. But one might ask and object, "Believe in the Lord Jesus Christ, and thou shalt be saved, and thy house," the meaning is this, "You yourself believing, shall be saved, and your house, *if* they believe;" and so, does this not only respect adults?

Answer. This cannot be the whole meaning, both because no house is said to be saved without the parents; and because this excludes infants from being said here to be saved, as well as from being said to believe. When therefore it is said, "Believe in the Lord Jesus Christ, and thou shalt be saved, and thy house," it is meant of some benefit (that is, *to be saved*) that shall redound to the house by the parent's profession to believe; which would not have redounded to it, if the parents did not make the profession, which must have respect principally to the infant children, which the parents have, or shall have afterwards (Genesis 17:7-8).

Add to this, that the house was *always* baptized, when the *parents* were baptized, but a house was not baptized without the parents. In this way, it is Lydia and her *household* baptized, the jailor and all his *household*, and Crispus with *all his house.* In differentiation to this, Cesar and his household were not baptized, even though some of his servants were because they were converted, where Lydia and Stephanas standing in a nearer relation to their houses, they being baptized, *their house and household were baptized also.* And so, all other houses said, or that may be said to be baptized in this way: if the parents are baptized so is their households, but no household is baptized without the parents, though a parent is sometimes mentioned and not the house, and sometimes the house, and not the parent (1 Corinthians 1:15-16). Now if any parents were baptized, their house, household, and all theirs were baptized, unless any of the adult refused for themselves, and no house or household were baptized. Where one or both of the parents were not so, it necessarily supposes some infants baptized in those baptize families, since they that were of age in it, who were baptized, and were baptized on their own account.

CHAPTER 2:
Objections Answered

Objection. But some may object: first, that *household* and *house* are not always said to be baptized with parents. It is not expressly said (Acts 18:8) that the house of Crispus was baptized; nor does the apostle (1 Corinthians 1:15) reckon it among those whom he enumerates to have baptized there; so neither is it expressly said of the house of Cornelius, that it was baptized.

Answer. Though this is true, yet so long as it is said of Cornelius, that he feared God with *all his house* (Acts 10:2) and had words sent to him, by which he and all his house should be saved (Acts 11:14), and of Crispus, that "he believed in the Lord *with all his house,*" and that Crispus and Cornelius themselves were baptized, it is all the same as if it had been expressly said, that all their house was baptized with them. No, further, though it is not expressly said of Zacchaeus, as well as that nobleman in John 4:53, that they were baptized, yet nothing can be more evident. For, though Christ did not baptize, yet his disciples did, and that as a great part of their employment during Christ's abode with them, for they baptized more than John (John 4:1). Now they baptizing so many, who should they baptize, if not them? And if them, why not their house and households? For if others in this way were qualified as baptized, themselves and

Chapter 2: Objections Answered

theirs, themselves and all their house, why not these, being qualified after the same manner, baptized they, themselves and their, themselves and all their house?

They were baptized is sufficiently confirmed by this, that though it is not expressly said in any of the gospels that the disciples of Christ baptized any particular persons or households, yet, when we come to the *Acts* of the apostles, by whose proceeding then we may see what was their practice all along before then. See also in 1 Corinthians 1:15 that we have a clear and particular account not only of the baptizing of single persons, but also of the baptizing with parents, their house and households. And this was always taken for granted, otherwise we can assign no reason why the apostle instancing in the baptizing of Crispus in the mentioning before citing 1 Corinthians 1:15, names him singularly, and does not mentions his house. There may be one reason why the apostle there says, that he was not sent to baptize, but to preach the gospel; namely, because if he had baptized all that he had converted, especially where parents and households were concerned, it would have hindered his preaching. But as Christ taught, and his disciples baptized, so the apostles might preach, and others under them sometimes baptize those whom they had converted. This is the way it was at Corinth, when many of the Corinthians, hearing Paul, believed. And so, we may suppose also that this occurred at Jerusalem after Peter's sermon (Acts 2:41).

And it is observed that when the apostle Paul gives us the names but of three which he remembered he had baptized of those many Corinthians, who are said to believe (Acts 18:8) that of two of them, Crispus and Stephanas, it is expressly said, *them and their house*. For, though in Corinthians it is singularly Crispus, as is observed before, yet in Acts it is *Crispus with all his house*; and if Gaius was Gaius the host, which supposes a household, and Gaius was Paul's host, which supposes a baptized household, then the same may be said of him as well.

Objection 2. Someone might say, but *house* and *household* are not always a Hebraism for *children* especially *infant children*; for 1 Corinthians 16:15, it is said "Ye know the house of Stephanas, that is the first fruits of Achaia, and that they have addicted themselves to the ministry of the saints." Now infants could not do this.

Answer. Divide house and parents here apart, and then none of the house could be infants; but as infants joined with parents are said (as in Jeremiah 35) to be *the house*, and to be spoken to (verse 2), to answer (verse 6), and to obey (verse 8, 10, 14, 16, 18), so infants may be said to be of the house of Stephanas, who attached themselves to the ministry of saints.

Objection 3. Someone may say, but it is said, John 4:1, "That Christ made and baptized more disciples than John," where "made" seems to imply only an adult.

Answer. If by *disciples* here is meant only those who did baptize, for Christ "baptized not," but his disciples did the baptizing, (that is, one another first, and then others) then they could be none but adults here. But if by *disciples* is meant also (as it must) those who were baptized, then it comprehends those "all men" said to come to Christ (John 3:26), such as those multitudes (Matthew 14:13-22) among whom many were children.

Objection 4. But it is said, Acts 8:12, "They were baptized, both men and women."

Answer. None can restrain these words, "men and women," to persons of such an exact age; neither because it is said, "men and women," does it also hinder infants from being understood, any more than saying, Nehemiah 8:3, "Ezra read the law to the men and women, and to all that could hear with understanding," hinders that their little ones were some in the assembly, which it did not, is cleared before as I previously showed you? When, therefore, it is said *men and women*, the sense is not, that none but of such an age, were or may be baptized, but that there was no distinction of sex in baptism, as there had been in circumcision (Galatians 3:28). For this, and that the things concerning the kingdom of God were preached to them (verse 12) being Samaritans, and that by it salvation came to their houses, and that of such was the kingdom of God, it was that there was great joy in the city (verse 8). And it being

Crispus singularly in the Corinthians, which in Acts is said as *Crispus with all his house*, it is a further confirmation of this sense, since infants may as well be couched under the terms of *men and women*, as Crispus' household *under his name*.

Objection 5. But what if there were no infant children in the households of Lydia, of the jailor, and of Crispus, so that they could not be baptized?

Answer. If there were no infant children in the households of Lydia, of the jailor, and of Crispus, they could not be baptized, then this objection seems to grant, that if there were, they were baptized. Now that there were infant children in those households (and none dare say there were not) appears from the following considerations.

1. That *house, household,* and *his,* (which are the words used) are, as proved before, when spoken of people, a Hebraism, so common and familiar to express children by, whether infants or adult, that there is none more frequent and ordinary.

2. That suppose these households are without infant children, and one may as well suppose all the houses and households, whose parents were baptized in those times, which could not be few, to be without infant children, which is something not to be supposed.

3. That a house being said to believe, to be saved, and to be baptized, where the parents are said to believe, to be saved, and to be baptized, and no house said to

believe, to be saved, and to be baptized, but whose parents are said to believe, to be saved, and to be baptized, it must be with respect to *their children*, especially their infant children, the adult being able to make profession *for themselves*.

And it being not only the apostles Peter and Paul, but all the disciples and apostles of Christ who baptized, that is to say, with parents, their *house* and *household*, and no house and household *without their parents*, can be nothing more plain than that it was the apostolical practice in baptizing parents and their households, to baptize their babes and infants.

Objection 6. But when Christ renewed his commission for baptizing (Matthew 28:19) he did not mentioned infants.

Answer. He then mentioned infants as much as adults, for he mentioned neither of them expressly.

Objection 7. But we have fresh examples of adult persons being baptized, and nothing of infants.

Answer. The express examples of those who the disciples and apostles of Christ baptized, are of two sorts; the one of particular adult persons, the other of parents *and their house*, (for a man and his house is parent and house) which being not only parents and adult, but parent and infants also, and as to baptism especially infants, as is made good all along as I have shown before. The baptizing of Lydia, the jailor, Crispus, and the like, and their house in conjunction with them, affords us as express examples of baptizing infants, as of baptizing any adult in the house, and consequently as of the baptizing of any other adult persons no matter who they were.

Objection 8. But Christ was not baptized in his infancy, and he knew when rightly to be baptized.

Answer. This makes no argument against baptizing infants; for as there were none then to baptize him so his baptism being in order to his ministry, into which he was not to enter by the law (which he came to fulfill, Matthew 5:17) until being about thirty years of age. He was not to be baptized until he had risen to that age. Besides, it is a question whether the baptism by John the Baptist, and the baptism of Christ by his disciples and apostles, were one and the same. For, though there was much said for it, and many instances of parallels drawn by which they are made to seem so, yet if it belonged to Christ ministerially to institute and ordain the sacraments of the New Testament, and if he could not ministerially do that until he was duly ordained and admitted into the function an office of his public ministry, which was not until his baptism by John, then John's baptism could not be a gospel sacrament, and if not a gospel sacrament, then his, and Christ's baptism, though they might agree in many other things, could not be one and the same.

Now Christ, not being baptized in his infancy, is no argument against baptizing infants. So, his baptism, and the baptism of John not being one and the same, makes the name of *Baptist* an improper distinction for all those who profess the baptism of Christ; as also that though the disciples of Christ, who before had been baptized into the baptism of John, as appears clearly by comparing John 1:35-37, 40, *etc.*, with John 4:1-2 and then which there is no clearer proof of their being baptized at all. Yet, the rebaptizing of any now is altogether groundless and unwarrantable.

Objection 9. But what benefit of baptism are infants capable of more, than they are capable of the benefit of the Lord's Table? Are they not as capable to receive a small quantity of bread and wine, as to be baptized?

Answer. This is to arraign the institutions of God, the profit of which, namely, that of circumcision, which included infants (Genesis 17:12). The apostle resolves to be "much every way, chiefly, because unto them were committed the oracles of God" (Romans 3:1-2). It arraigns also the commands of God mentioned before (Deuteronomy 31:11-13; Joel 2:12), and the express practice of the apostles, who when they baptized parents, baptized their house, and household; not so when they administered to them the Lord's Supper, it being not said there, "a man and his house," but, "let a man examine *himself.*"

Objection 10. But churches by means of paedobaptism become unholy and the unholiest of churches.

If churches become unholy by means of paedobaptism, then by what means did the primitive churches become unholy, with all the unholiness that is charged on them in the several epistles directed to them before, and in the Revelations, if it was by means of paedobaptism? Paedobaptism was in use in those times. So, if it was not by means of paedobaptism, then those in the church may become unholy by some other means. And if history does not do any wrong to the churches of the *antipaedobaptists*, they have not been so holy as *they* should have been. Now by what means did they come to be unholy, and unholiest? All those who were baptized in their infancy, if they do not answer the profession of faith and of a good conscience where they were baptized into, but afterwards make a shipwreck of that profession, and persist in it, then, "it had been better for them not to have known the way of righteousness, than after they have known it, to turn from the holy commandment once delivered to them." But it is not an argument why none but adult people should be baptized, for these also may make a defection from the faith, unless we will confute all experience. And then what way or course may, or ought to be taken with them on this occasion? The same may be taken with others on the same principles, and so Christianity and holiness are

Chapter 2: Objections Answered

preserved and secured in the churches of God as much this way, as it is pretended it may be in the other.

CHAPTER 3:
Two Resolutions

But there remains two things yet to be resolved; in resolving them it will be proved, that parents, and parents *only*, where they may be had, have right to present their children to God in baptism.

Question 1. The first, how do infants covenant, and engage to be God's people, or take Christ to be their Lord in baptism?

Answer. By their parents, who having first given themselves to the Lord, are bound to give and dedicate their children, both infants and adult, as their seed to him as well. And it was for this cause that no house was baptized *without the parents*; and adult covenanting and engaging for themselves, and the parents for their infants. The parents were doing that which they needed for their infants. They are like Joshua, resolving that he and his house would serve the Lord, while the infants promising by their parents, is as we may so say, as Levi paying tithes in the loins of Abraham.

And though that may be verified of infants, when their parents covenant for them in baptism, which Christ said to Peter, "What I do thou knowest not now." This line of thinking cannot be a bar to this practice because of that promise, "but thou shalt know hereafter" as being applicable to them, as it was to him.

And truly, they who go about to dispute themselves and others out of infant baptism by such arguments saying, "How do infants know that their parents covenant for them? And how can any after infancy tell what engagement lies on them by it?" May as well say, "how do we know who was the Father that begat us, or the Mother that brought us forth?" And so, they cast off that great commandment with promise, "Honour thy Father and thy Mother."

Question 2. The second is, why then are not parents, but others required in their stead, to answer for their children baptism?

Answer. Some have thought, that requiring of others, instead of the parents, to answer for their children in baptism was not brought into a canon until the clergy was prohibited marriage, and it may be so. But waving that the usual answer is, that however parents might be chiefly concerned in this at first, yet because parents might be taken away by death, driven away by persecution, or by some other means necessarily detained, when their children were to be baptized, the church does not exclude any title which the children have by the right of the parents. For, the sponsors may be supposed to appear in a threefold capacity. First, as representing the parents offering up the children to baptism, and by challenging it on their behalf. Secondly, by representing the children in the answers that are made at baptism. Thirdly, in their own capacity, when they promise to take care of the good education of the children in the principles of the Christian faith.

But though this may be done in defect of the parents, yet that parents when they may be had, should be quite jostled out by these, who were taken in only to supply their defects, seems not only to undervalue, yet oppose the wisdom of the first times, and resembles too much *the setting light* by father and mother, complained of in Ezekiel 22:7. "In thee have they set light by father and mother: in the midst of thee have they dealt by oppression with the stranger: in thee have they vexed the fatherless and the widow."

And where it is fairly pretended, that though one of the reasons (in other words, the perfection of those times) which made sureties more necessary in the first ages of the Christian Church, has long since ceased; yet that they are continued for good ends, as (not only to offer up, represent and promise, but) to covenant on the children's behalf, and secure the church that they may be brought to confirmation, and own their covenant afterwards.

These are reasons why there should be some sureties for infants; but none at all, why others rather than the parents, but altogether on the contrary. For, parents are not only much more responsible for all those good ends, but are confessedly those who were chiefly made use of in the first ages of the Christian church, until the persecution of those times cut them off. Now if persecution was one main thing that afterwards hindered parents, and that was a persecution so to do, why it should be thought of as a thing expedient in itself to hinder them now, by still requiring others in their stead. The reason is very difficult to resolve.

Nor is it so easy and small a matter to be a sponsor, or surety in this case, as many, it may be, make it to be (Ecclesiastes 5:2-8); nor a charge to be taken so rashly, and inconsiderately, as we may fear is done by the most. What parents may do for their own children, who are taken into covenant with them, is one thing; and what they may do for the children of others, who do not stand in that relation with them, is another. Every Christian is obliged more or less, if not as a witness, yet as a monitor, to help each other in their faith and manners. But for any to covenant with God, to promise and vow in the presence of God, and of his people solemnly assembled, to be such or such one's particular Christian monitor, and in their own capacity to promise as a surety, to take care of their good education in the principles of the Christian faith, not being their parents, or where the parents may be had, is a thing of a higher nature, and not without absolute necessity, to be either required, or undertaken.

The use of sureties should be so early in the Christian Church, as some pretend, that it is not easy to fix the time of its beginning; or, that it should be so ancient, as some think, among the Jews; as the time of

Isaiah, who took to himself as a witness to record such a thing (Isaiah 8:2).

Yet what are sureties? The time of whose beginning it is not easy to fix, to those made use of from the beginning. Or what are witnesses to sureties? Were witnesses anciently sureties? Or must we use sureties, because the prophet took unto himself witnesses?

And as to the reason of this, is it to offer up, dedicate, and devote children to God, (by their ministry, whose office it is) and represent them in answers to be made in baptism? Who are more proper for these than the parents, whose they are, who are parties with them, and who must answer in some respects to God for them?

Is it to promise, vow, and covenant on their behalf? Who are more fit for this than the parents themselves, with whom the covenant is made for themselves and theirs, and without which, sureties, and all their promising, vowing, and covenanting would signify nothing; children having no right to baptism, from promising, vowing and covenanting of others. For, the children of infidels might have right, but as the parents themselves promise, vow and covenant for them. And if other sureties challenge on the parents right, why not make the parents themselves challenge on their own?

Is it to undertake for the children's good education in the principles of the Christian faith? Who are laid under such strict commands, bound in such indispensable obligations, charged with that care, and trust, and furnished with those for advantageous opportunities for its discharge, as the parents (Psalm 78:5, 6; Proverbs 19:18; and 29:27)? Does not even nature itself teach us? And to whom has God said at anytime concerning the children of others, as to parents concerning theirs, "Thou shalt teach them diligently unto thy children, and shalt talk of them when thou sittest in thy house, and when thou walkest by the way, and when thou liest down, and when thou risest up," (Deuteronomy 6:7). And when the apostle says, "Ye fathers, provoke not your children to wrath; but bring them up in the nurture and admonition of the Lord," (Ephesians 6:4), of whom principally does he say this, of the fathers of their flesh or of some others?

And for the security of the church, that the children may be brought to confirmation, and own their covenant, where are the parents less responsible, or more insufficient than the sureties? It is the parents that God looks after; and if they bring up their children for him, do they not bring them up for the church? What does the church need than any other sureties? Or, where is it better secured by them? As for sureties, it is well known, that any are generally accepted. Besides, some do but stand for other sureties; and some are sureties for the children of several families. And what is there more common, than for the younger sort of sureties to be removed into other habitations and abodes? And for those of greater years, to have charged of their own, which are sufficient to take up all their care and endeavours? Moreover, are not families very often changing their dwellings? How then, it may be again asked, is the church more or better secured by sureties, than it would be by parents? Whose security, if it was taken in this way, would be something, where that of sureties is, besides its uncertainty, usually but in complement, having a form of godliness, but little or nothing of its power. So that if it should be demanded, what advantage, as to these things, has the church? Or, what profit is there by them to the parents, or their children? Or, what glory would it give to God? It would be hard to say "much in every way." Besides, is not filthiness and uncleanness by this covered and masked? Which it may be hoped would be shamed out of, if only parents were required personally to present their infants.

To sum up everything, are any people proper and competent to represent the children of others, to offer them up in baptism to God, to make a promise for their virtuous and religious education, to covenant with God for them, secure the church, and receive the charge and exhortation given in their behalf? And must they not be much more proper and competent for their own? Or, if they are not proper and competent for their own, how do they come to be proper and competent for the children of others?

This does not hinder anything when others may hand children from the parents to the minister; or stand as witnesses of their baptism. So, they do not proceed to serve in things appertaining to the parents.

For the service and worship of God requiring personal attendance, and it not being in the power of any to require the performance of one man's religious duty of another, or of one man, to perform another man's religious duty for him. So that if any should require any man to go to the church, serve God, partake of the Lord's Supper for another, or, if any should pretend that he does all these things, by another's doing it for him, it would be useless. Even so to offer up, devote, and dedicate children to God in baptism, to covenant for them, and in this solemnly to promise and vow their religious education, all which are part of the Christian religion, and divine worship, is no discharge to the parents, whose part and duty it is, let them pretend what they will of doing it by others, unless they themselves perform it. And therefore, that parents should be required and necessitated to do it by others, or it must not be done at all, when they themselves may do it, is a matter that deserves the most serious consideration of those who do not challenge a dispensing or infallible power.

If any should think that parents therefore may not answer, promise, vow or covenant for their children in baptism, because this would be to serve God for them.

It does not follow. For when parents answer, promise, vow and covenant in their children's name, they do not perform their children's duty for them, but they do engage them to it, and they perform their own duty before God. And so far as the parents act of giving up and dedicating their children to God in a way of covenant, and in this answering for them, is a work of necessity and mercy, it is no more a performing of their children's duty, or a serving of God for them, than praying to God for them, or as being their mouth to God in praise is.

To conclude: since suretyship, and making vows for others, is no light and easy matter, that doing this for children, being in things of the greatest moment, and to God who will not be mocked, is not a small thing to consider. It is not in our power to substitute one for another, or others in our stead to serve God for us, nor safe to trifle with sacred things. How well would it be if that suretyship, which is founded on covenant-right, accommodated with the greatest advantages, most expedient in itself, most competent for all the good ends of suretyship, most unquestionable, and which was from the beginning, in other words, the parent was always required. In taking up this responsibility by parents, if such, whose ministerial calling and employment it is, would super-add their endeavours by a frequent assisting of the parents on all convenient occasions, remembering them always, that "he is not a Christian which is one outwardly" (Romans 2:28-29) "neither is that baptism which is outward in the flesh; but he is Christian which is one inwardly, and baptism is that of the heart in the spirit, and not in the letter, whose praise is not of men, but of God." How useful might this be, and more religious than for them, waving the parents, to bind heavy burdens and grievous to be born and lay them on other men's shoulders, and they themselves not move them with one of their fingers?

"Now the God of patience and consolation grant us to be like-minded one towards another, according to Christ Jesus; that we may with one mind and one mouth glorify God, even the Father of our Lord Jesus Christ," (Romans 15:5-6). *Amen.*

FINIS.

Appendix

As to Christ being baptized when 30 years old, at the beginning of his ministry, (mentioned before) and also about the differences an agreements of Christ's baptism and John's, let the inquisitive reader peruse and pause on those brief, but excellent points on which that diligent reader of the sacred scriptures, Mr. Samuel Clark, has lately given us, in his notes on Matthew 3:6, 16. Though I confess that Christ's plea for his being baptized by John, [in this way "to fulfill all righteousness"] I cannot yet say that I understand it in its utmost reach and force to my full satisfaction. That Christ was bound to (and so must) fulfill the law of Moses, and John's prophetic mission, and the whole law of mediation which his Father laid him under, and he so voluntarily obliged himself to, admits no doubt, and needs no proof. But what particular law Christ here respected as to this instance, I cannot say I yet fully know.

As to sponsors, (godfathers and godmothers) 1. Let them be serious, and devoted people to God and Christ, themselves, 2. Capable of receiving and likely and willing to fulfill this trust. And, 3. then appear and stand as the substitutes and representatives of absent parents through necessity; or pro-parents, whose parents are dead, or manifestly give their children wholly to them, or, as in conjunction and concurrence with the parents, for the more effectual Christian education of the baptized children. And then less may be said against them, and more for them than otherwise. And then their testimony will be more credible, that persons offering their seed to God, are such as very probably have a right thereto. That the persons offered are baptized; and that in case the parents die, or deny the faith, or prove grossly negligent as to the performance of their trust, care will yet be taken about the fit Christian education of their baptized seed. But why parents (where they can) should not solemnly and personally *offer their own* natural seed to God, and personally profess and promise, I do not know. Seeing this renews their Christian profession, reinforces their Christian obligations and advantages on themselves; hands down the essentials of Christianity from age to age, calls other parents to reflect upon themselves as to their Christian advantages, performances, and concerns; and quickens all the baptized to their work and hope.

    I will not vouch for every word and thing in this, or any mere human book; but I do not think it is lost labor or time to have this read, this small tract.

M.S.

Appendix 2

A Catechism of Infant Inclusion in the Covenant of Grace
by C. Matthew McMahon, Ph.D., Th.D.

The early church and the historic Reformed community believed they *should* baptize infants. But why? Matthew Sylvester has already treated the answer to this quite nicely, and he's done so with a sharp, penetrating knife that has cut away that age old excuse of not having a "plain text" copying the Sadducees who erred not knowing the Scriptures, and denied the power of God. Sylvester mentioned that baptism has to do with *covenant*. Keep in mind that infant baptism, as a studied doctrine overall, is the last five minutes of a ten-hour study on covenant theology.[1] Most faulty inquirers will attempt to work backwards making this doctrine a difficult one to understand, and falling into the same condemnation that Christ gave the erring Sadducees. Consequently, maybe this short catechism will aid that student in seeing more clearly some of the reasoning behind what Sylvester has already taught.

---

[1] See my works "A Simple Overview of Covenant Theology" and "Covenant Theology Made Easy" for introductions to the subject matter. Puritan Publications has a number of works published on this subject, many of which are at great length, and some, which are shorter more manageable books.

Appendix 2

In reading this catechism, my only requirement of you, reader, is in dealing with this often confused and yet glorious doctrine that magnifies both Christ and his word, that you completely read through the entire *Catechism* and the historical quotes given at the end to appreciate the historic and biblical position on this topic (it may even be beneficial to read it over more than once). Doctrines that are new or difficult to understand have a tendency to shake people up if they do not read all the way through what is being said (where people misunderstand the doctrine because of a lack of information, or a twisting of what is being said, or selectively citing the information as has been the case in the past on this issue).

THE CATECHISM

Question 1: Are children of believers included in the Covenant of Grace?
Answer: Yes, children are included in the Covenant of Grace, and the visible church.[2]

Question 2: Upon what grounds are children part of the Covenant of Grace?

---

[2] Genesis 17:1-14; Matthew 19:14; 1 Corinthians 7:14.

Answer: By two reasons: the promises of God[3] and the command of God.[4]

Question 3: What is the promise of God?
Answer: That God would be a God to Abraham and his descendants after him for an everlasting covenant,[5] and that the children of believers are entitled to such a promise since it was made with Abraham and his children, Christ Jesus being *mystically* considered as Abraham's Seed and the entire Christian church considered in him.[6]

Question 4: What is the command of God?
Answer: The command of God compels all believing parents to have the sign of the covenant of God placed on their children.[7]

Question 5: How are the promises of God applicable to children since they are born sinful and depraved?
Answer: The promises of God are applicable to the children of believers since Christian parents presumptively believe their children are regenerate

---

[3] Genesis 15:1; 17:7; Acts 2:39; Galatians 3:18; 2 Peter 1:4.
[4] Gen. 17:10-12; Acts 21:21; Matthew 28:19.
[5] Genesis 17:7; 17:13; 17:19; Psalm 105:9-10; Hebrews 13:20.
[6] Genesis 17:7; 26:24; Isaiah 55:3; Jeremiah 32:40; Joel 2:28; Matthew 22:32; Acts 3:25; Romans 4:13.
[7] Gen. 17:23; Joshua 5:3; Luke 2:21; Acts 21:20; Matthew 3:6; Acts 16:15; 16:33; 1 Corinthians 10:2.

Appendix 2

based on the Word of God and the command of God, and presume God to be their Savior as He promised.[8]

Question 6: Does this presumption (that the children of believers are regenerate) negate the reality that these children are conceived in sin, or demonstrate an inconsistency with Total Depravity?

Answer: No. Children of believing parents are conceived in sin, corrupt, depraved and in need of salvation,[9] but their parents presume them to be regenerate, yet are actually regenerate by sovereign election at a time only God knows, if at all;[10] they are to be considered Christians by their parents based on the promise God has made to them, that God will in fact save them and be a God to them, unless God in His command is liar;[11] and this view is not inconsistent with Total Depravity since sovereign grace is the means by which God will regenerate and save a child.[12]

Question 7: Are infants of believing parents to be considered Christians?

Answer: Yes.

---

[8] Genesis 17:7; Acts 2:39; Ezekiel 36:24.
[9] Genesis 6:5; Psalm 51:5; Romans 3:10-18.
[10] Luke 1:15; Ephesians 1:9.
[11] Genesis 17:7; Acts 2:39; 16:33.
[12] Romans 4:16; Ephesians 1:3-10; 2:8-10.

Question 8: Why are infants of believing parents to be considered Christians?

Answer: Based on the command and promise of God, they are to be distinguished from the visible world,[13] and are united with believers in the church,[14] being federally holy before God[15] and marked by the covenant sign of circumcision[16] (as in the case of the patriarchs and Israelites) or of baptism[17] (as in the case of the fulfillment of the Covenant of Grace realized in Christ).

Question 9: Are infants of believing parents to be considered as members of the invisible church or the visible church or both?

Answer: Infants of believing parents are *presumed* to be in the invisible church[18] and are actually part of the visible church.[19]

Question 10: Are all children of believing parents infallibly saved?

Answer: No. They are presumed saved by the parents based on the promises, but may in fact demonstrate their

---

[13] Genesis 3:15; Ezekiel 16:20-21; 1 Corinthians 2:12.
[14] Ephesians 2:19; 3:15.
[15] Malachi 2:15; 1 Corinthians 7:14.
[16] Genesis 17:10; Leviticus 12:3.
[17] Ezekiel 36:25; Matthew 28:19; Acts 2:39; 16:33.
[18] Genesis 17:7; Acts 2:39.
[19] Rom. 15:8; Exod. 12:48; Gen. 34:14; Acts 21:21.

apostasy after the age of discretion,[20] showing themselves in need of saving faith.[21]

Question 11: Is this contradictory?
Answer: No. Christian parents presume the regeneration of their children based on the precepts of the Word of God and do not have prior information concerning the decreed eternal destiny of any fellow human being, much less their own children.

Question 12: Is the account of when Abraham circumcised Ishmael inconsistent with the view that infants of believing parents should be presumed regenerate (though he knew that God told him Ishmael would be cast out)?
Answer: No. The sign is administered by way of *promise and command*. Though the promise would be realized in Isaac,[22] the command still rendered Abraham duty-bound to administer the sign of the covenant on Ishmael,[23] sealing the curses of the covenant upon him as a reprobate.[24] [23]

Question 13: In presuming that infants of believing parents are regenerate, does this mean they have an

---

[20] Genesis 25:34; Hebrews 10:29.
[21] John 1:12; 5:47; 6:29; Romans 1:17.
[22] Genesis 21:12.
[23] Genesis 17:12.
[24] Deuteronomy 11:26-28.

active and actual faith whereby they do good works, understand the Word of God, and meditate on it?

Answer: Infants do not have actual faith, but habitual faith, or *faith of habit*, for as an acorn possesses in it all the properties of a giant oak tree, so infants possess all the properties necessary for faith as "seed faith" (a faith implanted in them by God and dormant until they reach an age in which they are able to rationally think); infants are unable to discern between their left hand and right hand,[25] not capable of outward acts of faith,[26] and not capable of hearing or meditating on the Word.[27]

Question 14: Are infants of believing parents part of the Kingdom of God?

Answer: Yes. Christ says the Kingdom of Heaven *belongs* to them,[28] which demonstrates that a real "seed faith" is in them since no one is able to enter the Kingdom of heaven without true faith.[29]

Question 15: Why does God desire Christian parents to presume their infants are regenerate?

---

[25] Deuteronomy 1:39; Isaiah 7:16; Jonah 4:11.
[26] Romans 12:1-2.
[27] Romans 10:17; Hebrews 11:16.
[28] Matthew 19:14.
[29] John 3:3, 5.

Answer: God desires that Christian parents *rely on his revealed* Word[30] which includes the children of believing parents in the Covenant of Grace

Question 16: May a child of believing parents, after the age of discretion or confirmation, ultimately be lost?
Answer: God may, by an eternal decree of reprobation, account them lost forever (which is different than His will of precept that Christians are to obey) such as in the case of Ishmael, Esau or others, who outwardly demonstrated their rebellion and reprobation.[31]

Question 17: Has God said that His will of precept concerning covenant children is equal to His will of decree concerning covenant children?
Answer: No. At no time has God said that His will of precept (the Word of God given to us in the Bible) is always the same or equal to His will of decree.[32]

Question 18: If God's will of decree is different at times than His will of precept, which shall Christians follow?
Answer: Christians are to obey God at His Word, and by His promises, and continue diligently in a constant state of considering whether they truly believe the promises

---

[30] Psalm 119:105; John 17:17.
[31] Exodus 19:5; Leviticus 26:14-16; Deuteronomy 11:13; Ezekiel 20:39; Zechariah 6:15; Romans 9:13; Hebrews 12:16; Galatians 4:24-25.
[32] Deuteronomy 29:29; Daniel 2:22.

of God or not,[33] which prompts them to sanctifying holiness,[34] and to diligence in teaching their children the Word of God as faithful parents.[35]

Question 19: Is the doctrine of the inclusion of infants in the Covenant of Grace, and therefore presuming their regeneration, new or novel, unknown to history?
Answer: No. The Early Church, the Reformers, the Confessions, English Puritanism, and Protestant Presbyterianism teach this up and through our present day. How might this be proven from history?

The following are a few selected quotes from church history:

John Calvin, "We ought, therefore, to consider, that just as in the case of Abraham, the father of the faithful, the righteousness of faith preceded circumcision, so today in the children of the faithful, the gift of adoption is prior to baptism." (Opera Quae Supersunt Omina, *Corpus Reformatorum*, Volume 35, Page 8.)

John Calvin, "...that the children of believers are not baptized, that they may thereby then become the children of God, as if they had been before aliens to the

---

[33] 2 Corinthians 13:5; John 5:38; 6:29.
[34] 1 Thessalonians 4:3.
[35] Proverbs 22:6; Deuteronomy 4:10, 6:7; Ephesians 6:4.

church; but, on the contrary, they are received into the Church by this solemn sign, since they already belonged to the body of Christ by virtue of the promise." (*Institutes of the Christian Religion*, 4:15:22. cf. 4:16:24.)

The French Confession, "We confess only two sacraments common to the whole Church, of which the first, baptism, is given as a pledge of our adoption; for by it we are grafted into the body of Christ, so as to be washed and cleansed by his blood, and then renewed in purity of life by his Holy Spirit. We hold, also, that although we are baptized only once, yet the gain that it symbolizes to us reaches over our whole lives and to our death, so that we have a lasting witness that Jesus Christ will always be our justification and sanctification. Nevertheless, although it is a sacrament of faith and penitence, yet as God receives little children into the Church with their fathers, we say, upon the authority of Jesus Christ, that the children of believing parents should be baptized."

Ulrich Zwingli, "The children of Christians are not less the children of God than their parents are, or than the children of Old Testament times were: but if they belong to God, who will refuse them baptism?" (Huldreich Zwingli's Werke, *Zweyten bandes erste Abtheilung* (Zurich, 1830), Page 245.)

Martin Bucer and Wolfgang Capito, "...baptism signified regeneration; that the children of believers are baptized because it is wrong to keep them from the fellowship and company of God's people those who should be truly considered His people." (Lewis Schenck, *The Presbyterian Doctrine of Children in the Covenant*, Page 28.)

Theodore Beza, "It cannot be the case that those who have been sanctified by birth and have been separated from the children of unbelievers, do not have the seed or germ of faith." (*Confessio Chrsitanae Fidei*, Book 4, Page 48.)

Henry Bullinger, "Since the young babes and infants of the faithful are in the number of reckoning of God's people, and partakers of the promise touching the purification through Christ; it followeth of necessity, that they are as well to be baptized, as they that be of perfect age which professes the Christian faith," (*Fifty Godly and Learned Sermons* (London, 1587) Page 382.

The Second Helvetic Confession, "We condemn the Anabaptists, who deny that newborn infants of the faithful are to be baptized. For according to evangelical teaching, of such is the Kingdom of God, and they are in the covenant of God. Why, then, should the sign of God's covenant not be given to them? Why should those who belong to God and are in his Church not be initiated by holy baptism?" (Chapter 20, *Of Holy Baptism.*)

Francis Turretin, "The orthodox occupy the middle ground between Anabaptism and the Lutherans. They deny actual faith to infants against the Lutherans and maintain a seminal or radical and habitual faith is to be ascribed to them against the Anabaptists. Here it is to be remarked before all things: that we do not speak of the infants of any parents whomsoever (even of infidels and heathen), but only of believers, or Christians and the covenanted. (*Institutes of Elenctic Theology*, Volume 2, Page 583.)

Peter Martyr Vermigli, "We assume that the children of believers are holy, as long as in growing up they do not demonstrate themselves to be estranged from Christ. We do not exclude them from the church, but accept them as members, with the hope that they are partakers of the divine election and have the grace and Spirit of Christ, even as they are the seed of saints. On that basis we baptize them." (Loci Communes, 4:8:7, cf. Robert Reymond's, *A New systematic Theology of the Christian Faith*, Page 946.)

The Belgic Confession, "Therefore we detest the error of the Anabaptists, who are not content with the one only baptism they have once received, and moreover condemn the baptism of the infants of believers, who we believe ought to be baptized and sealed with the sign of the covenant, as the children in Israel formerly were circumcised upon the same promises which are made unto our children. And indeed Christ shed His blood no less for the washing of the children of believers than for adult persons; and therefore they ought to receive the sign and sacrament of that which Christ has done for them; as the Lord commanded in the law that they should be made partakers of the sacrament of Christ's suffering and death shortly after they were born, by offering for them a lamb, which was a sacrament of Jesus Christ. Moreover, what circumcision was to the Jews, baptism is to our children. And for this reason St. Paul calls baptism the circumcision of Christ." (Article 34.)

The Heidelberg Catechism, "Q74: Are infants also to be baptized? A74: Yes, for since they, as well as their parents, belong to the covenant and people of God, and through the blood of Christ both redemption from sin and the Holy Ghost, who works faith, are promised to them no less than to their parents, they are also by Baptism, as a sign of the covenant, to be ingrafted into the Christian Church, and distinguished from the children of unbelievers, as was done in the Old Testament by circumcision, in place of which in the New Testament Baptism is appointed. (Lord's Day 27.)

The 1647 Westminster Assembly, "That it [baptism] is instituted by our Lord Jesus Christ: That it is a seal of the Covenant of Grace, of our ingrafting into Christ, and of our union with him, of remission of sins, regeneration, adoption, and life eternal: That the water, in baptism, representeth and signifieth both the blood of Christ, which taketh away all guilt of sin, original and actual; and the sanctifying virtue of the Spirit of Christ against the dominion of sin, and the corruption of our sinful nature: That baptizing, or sprinkling and washing with water, signifieth the cleansing from sin by the blood and for the merit of Christ, together with the mortification of sin, and rising from sin to newness of life, by virtue of the death and resurrection of Christ: That the promise is made to believers and their seed; and that the seed and posterity of the faithful, born within the church, have, by their birth, interest in the covenant, and right to the seal of it, and to the outward privileges of the church, under the gospel, no less than the children of Abraham in the time of the Old Testament; the Covenant of Grace, for substance, being the same; and the grace of God, and the consolation of believers, more plentiful than before: That the Son of God admitted little children into his presence, embracing and blessing them, saying, For of such is the kingdom of God: That children, by baptism, are solemnly received into the bosom of the visible church, distinguished from the world, and them that are without, and united with believers; and that all who are baptized in the name of Christ, do renounce, and by their baptism are bound to fight against the devil, the world, and the flesh: That they are Christians, and federally holy before baptism, and therefore are they baptized." (*The Directory of Public Worship.*)[36]

The Thirty-nine Articles of Religion, "Baptism is not only a sign of profession, and mark of difference, whereby Christian men are discerned from others that be not christened, but it is also a sign of Regeneration or New-Birth, whereby, as by an instrument, they that receive Baptism rightly are grafted into the Church; the promises of the forgiveness of sin, and of our adoption to be the sons of God by the Holy Ghost, are visibly signed and sealed; Faith is confirmed, and Grace increased by virtue of prayer unto God. The Baptism of young Children is in any wise to be retained in the Church, as most agreeable with the institution of Christ." (Article XXVI, *Of Baptism.*)

Zacharias Ursinus, "First, all that belong to the covenant and church of God are to be baptized. But the children of Christians, as well as adults, belong to the covenant and church of God. Therefore, they are to be baptized, as well as adults. Secondly, those are not to be excluded

---

[36] Make note that the 1647 Westminster Confession of Faith does not make a distinction between baptism and infant baptism as to the effects or use of baptism. They make no distinction between subjects of baptism in the use of it on those subjects.

from baptism to whom the benefit of remission of sins, and of regeneration, belongs. But this benefit belongs to the infants of the church; for redemption from sin, by the blood of Christ, and the Holy Ghost, the author of faith, is promised to them no less than to the adult. Therefore, they ought to be baptized." (*Commentary on the Heidelberg Catechism*, (1st American Edition, 1851, Pages 366-367.)

William Ames, "The infants of believers are not to be forbidden this sacrament. First, because, if they are partakers of any grace, it is by virtue of the Covenant of Grace and so both the covenant and the first seal of the covenant belong to them. Second, the covenant in which the faithful are now included is clearly the same as the covenant made with Abraham, Rom. 4:11; Gal. 3:7-9 — and this expressly applied to infants. Third, the covenant as now administered to believers brings greater and fuller consolation than it once could, before the coming of Christ. But if it pertained only to them and not to their infants, the grace of God and their consolation would be narrower and more contracted after Christ's appearing than before. Fourth, baptism supplants circumcision, Col. 2:11-12; it belongs as much to the children of believers as circumcision once did. Fifth, in the very beginning of regeneration, whereof baptism is a seal, man is merely passive. Therefore, no outward action is required of a man when he is baptized or circumcised (unlike other sacraments); but only a passive receiving. Infants are, therefore, as capable of participation in this sacrament, so far as its chief benefit is concerned, as adults." (*The Marrow of Theology*, Page 211.)

John Bradford, "In baptism is required God's election, if the child be an infant, or faith, if he be of age." (*The Writings of John Bradford*, Banner of Truth Trust, Carlisle, 1979, Volume 2, Page 290.)

Herman Witsius, "Here certainly appears the extraordinary love of our God, in that as soon as we are born, and just as we come from our mother, he hath commanded us to be solemnly brought from her bosom, as it were, into his own arms, that he should bestow upon us, in the very cradle, the tokens of our dignity and future kingdom;...that, in a word, he should join us to himself in the most solemn covenant from our most tender years: the remembrance of which, as it is glorious and full of consolation to us, so in like manner it tends to promote Christian virtues, and the strictest holiness, through the whole course of our lives." (*The Economy of the Covenants Between God and Man*, (London, 1868) Volume 3, Book 4, Chapter 18, Page 1219.)

John Owen, "The end of his message and of his coming was, that those to whom he was sent might be "blessed with faithful Abraham," or that "the blessing of Abraham," promised in the covenant, "might come upon them," Galatians 3:9, 14. To deny this, overthrows the whole relation between the old testament and the new, the veracity of God in his promises, and all the properties of the Covenant of Grace, mentioned 2 Samuel 23:5...Infants are made for and are capable of eternal glory or misery, and must fall, dying infants, into one of these estates for ever. All infants are born in a state of sin, wherein they are spiritually dead and under the curse. Unless they are regenerated or born again, they must all perish inevitably, John 3:3. Their regeneration is the grace where of baptism is a sign or token. Wherever this is, there baptism ought to be administered. It follows hence unavoidably that infants who die in their infancy have the grace of regeneration, and consequently as good a right unto baptism as believers themselves...In brief, a participation of the seal of the covenant is a spiritual blessing. This the seed of believers was once solemnly invested in by God himself. This privilege he hath nowhere revoked, though he hath changed the outward sign; nor hath he granted unto our children any privilege or mercy in lieu of it now under the gospel, when all grace and privileges are enlarged to the utmost. His covenant promises concerning them, which are multiplied, were confirmed by Christ as a true messenger and minister; he gives the grace of baptism unto many of them, especially those that die in their infancy, owns children to belong unto his kingdom, esteems them disciples, appoints households to be baptized without exception. And who shall now rise up, and withhold water from them?" (*Works*, Volume 16, Banner of Truth Trust (Carlisle, 1988) Pages 335-337.)

Samuel Rutherford, "It is clear that infants have their share of salvation, and by covenant it must be...And this promise made to Abraham belongs to them all..." (*The Covenant of Life Opened*, 1642(?), Pages 83, 104-105.)

Richard Sibbes, "Therefore God, intending a comfortable enlargement of the Covenant of Grace to Abraham, extends it to his seed: "I will be the God of thy seed." It is a great blessing for God to be the God of our seed. It is alluded to by St Peter in the New Testament, "The promise is made to you and to your children," Acts ii. 39. But what if they have not baptism, the seal of the covenant? That doth not prejudice their salvation. God hath appointed the sacraments to be seals for us, not for himself. He himself keepeth his covenant, whether we have the seal or no, so long as we neglect it not. Therefore we must not think if a child die before the sacrament of baptism, that God will not keep his covenant. They have the sanctity, the holiness of the covenant. You know what David said of his child, "I shall go to it, but it shall not return to me;" and yet it died before it was circumcised. You know they were forty years in the wilderness, and were not circumcised. Therefore the sacrament is not of absolute necessity to salvation. So he is the God of our children from the conception and birth." (*Works of Richard Sibbes*, Volume 6, Banner of Truth Trust, (Carlisle 1983), Page 22.)

Ezekiel Hopkins, "Certainly, since they [infants of believing parents] are in covenant with God; since they are the members of Christ, being members of His body, the Church; since they are sanctified and regenerated, so far forth as their natures are ordinarily capable of, without a miracle; we have all the reason in the world conformably to conclude, that all such die in the Lord, and are forever happy and blessed with Him." (Works, Volume 2 page 326.)

Thomas Goodwin, "The children of godly parents are called the inheritance of the Lord, because he is the owner of them as his elect and chosen, among whom his possession and his peculiar people lie...The children of believing parents, at least their next and immediate seed, even of us Gentiles now under the Gospel, are included by God within the covenant of Grace, as well as Abraham's or David's seed within that covenant of theirs." (*Works*, Volume 9, Page 426-427.)

Thomas Manton, "If they die before they come to the use of reason, you have no cause to doubt of their salvation.

God is their God. Gen. 17:7, "I will establish my covenant between me and thee, and thy seed after thee in their generations, for an everlasting covenant, to be a God unto thee, and to thy seed after thee;" compared with Gal. 3:14, "That the blessing of Abraham might come on the gentiles through Jesus Christ, that we might receive the promise of the Spirit through faith." And they never lived to disinherit themselves. As we judge of the slip according to the stock, till it live to bring forth fruit of its own, so here. (Manton's Complete *Works*, Volume 18, Page 91.)

John Brown of Haddington, "None but regenerated persons have a right to baptism before God...None but such as appear truly regenerated have a right to baptism before men...The infants of parents, one or both visible saints, have a right to baptism before the church...The children of believers are in covenant with God...Infants, such as Christ could carry in his arms, are members of the Kingdom of God. And if members, why deny them the primary seal of membership?" (*Systematic Theology*, Page 538.)

Alexander Whyte, "Baptism does not effect our engrafting into Christ, it only signifies and seals it." (*Commentary on the Shorter Catechism*, Page 181.) [Note, there is no distinction between adults and children, or infants, in the Westminster Confession at all on this issue, except by age, and the Directory of Public Worship makes it abundantly clear what they mean by the institution and how it should be administered.]

Robert Shaw, "...for infants of believing parents are born within the covenant, and so are Christians and visible church members; and by baptism this right of theirs is acknowledged, and they are solemnly admitted to the privileges of church membership." (*An Exposition of the Confession of Faith*, 1845, Page 285.)

J. W. Alexander, "But O how we neglect that ordinance! Treating children in the Church, just as if they were out of it. Ought we not daily to say (in its spirit) to our children, "You are Christian children, you are Christ's, you ought to think and feel and act as such! And on this plan carried out, might we not expect more early fruit of the grace than by keeping them always looking forward to a point of time at which they shall have new hearts and join the church? I am distressed with long harbored misgivings on this point." (*Forty Years' Familiar Letters*, Volume 2, Page 25.)

Lyman Atwater, "If our children are in precisely the same position as others, why baptize them?" (Children of the covenant and their part in the Lord, Biblical

Repertory and Princeton Review, Volume 35, No. 4 (October, 1863), Page 622.)

Lewis Schenck, "The Reformed Church has always believed, on the basis of God's immutable promise, that all children of believers dying in infancy were saved...in other words, all admission to the visible church was on the basis, not of an infallible evidence of regeneration, since no one could read the heart, but on the basis of presumption that those admitted were the true children of God." (*The Presbyterian Doctrine of Children in the Covenant*, (Phillipsburg, 2003) Page 118.

Benjamin B. Warfield, "All baptism is inevitably administered on the basis not of knowledge but of presumption and if we must baptize on presumption the whole principle is yielded; and it would seem that we must baptize all whom we may fairly presume to be members of Christ's body." (The Polemics of Infant Baptism, *The Presbyterian Quarterly* (April, 1899), Page 313.

Henry Van Dyke, "If the baptism of infants does not signify and seal "regeneration and engrafting into Christ," in the same sense and to the same extent as in the case of adults, we have no right to administer it to infants." (*The Church: Her Ministry and Sacraments*, Page 74.)

Abraham Kuyper, "That children of believers are to be considered as recipients of efficacious grace, in whom the work of efficacious grace has already begun. That when dying before having attained to years of discretion, they can only be regarded as saved. Of course [he adds] Calvinists never declared that these things were necessarily so. As they never permitted themselves to pronounce official judgment on the inward state of an adult, but left the judgment to God, so they have never usurped the right to pronounce on the presence or absence of spiritual life in infants. They only stated how God would have us consider such infants, and this consideration based on the divine word made it imperative to look upon their infant children as elect and saved, and to treat them accordingly." (Abraham Kuyper, "Calvinism and Confessional Review," *The Presbyterian Quarterly*, Vol. IV, No. 18 (October, 1891), Art. I, pp. 602-503; cf. 604.)

Charles Hodge, "The historic Reformed Doctrine which may be identified with that of John Calvin was as follows: Membership in the invisible church meant vital union with Christ, or regeneration by the Holy Spirit. Since the word presume meant to admit a thing to be, or to receive a thing as true, before it could be known as such from its phenomena or manifestations, the presumption that an infant was a member of the invisible church meant that it was believed to be engrafted into Christ and regenerated before it gave any ordinary evidences of the fact." (*The Church Membership of Infants*, Page 375.)

Lewis Berkhof and the Conclusions of Utrecht, "It may be well to quote in this connection the first half of the fourth point of the Conclusions of Utrecht, which were adopted by our Church in 1908. We translate this as follows: "And, finally, as far as the fourth point, that of presumptive regeneration, is concerned. Synod declares that, according to the confession of our Churches, the seed of the covenant must, in virtue of the promise of God, be presumed to be regenerated and sanctified in Christ, until, as they grow up, the contrary appears from their life or doctrine; that it is, however, less correct to say that baptism is administered to the children of believers on the ground of their presumptive regeneration, since the ground of baptism is the command and the promise of God; and that further the judgment of charity, with which the Church presumes the seed of the covenant to be regenerated, by no means intends to say that therefore each child is really regenerated, since the Word of God teaches that they are not all Israel that are of Israel, and it is said of Isaac: in him shall thy seed be called (Rom. 9:6-7), so that in preaching it is always necessary to insist on serious self-examination, since only those who shall have believed and have been baptized will be saved." (*Systematic Theology*, Page 640.)

A. A. Hodge, "But baptism does not ordinarily confer grace in the first instance, but presupposes it." (*Outlines of Theology*, Page 629.)

John Murray, "Baptized infants are to be received as the children of God and treated accordingly." (*Christian Baptism*, Page 59.)

Robert Booth, "If the children of believers are embraced by the promises of the covenant, as certainly they are, then they must also be entitled to receive the initial sign of the covenant, which is baptism." (*Children of the Promise*, P&R Publishing, Page 29.)

Robert Reymond, "I think I have shown that infants of believing parents are to be viewed as members of and under the governance and protection of Christ's church and should be treated as such...Accordingly, all present at any and every infant baptism are admonished to "look back to their baptism," to repent of their sins against the covenant, and to "improve and make right use of their baptism...the Directory [of Public Worship] envisions, as Jones rightly states, "a dynamic, life-long relationship between the infants saving faith and Christian walk, on the one hand, and his baptism on the other." (*A New*

Systematic Theology of the Christian Faith, Pages 948-49.)

John Knox, "The conviction of the writers of that Book of Common Order, was thus the Biblical perception that the children of believers are Christians already, before being baptized in their infancy."

Genevan Book of Church Order, still describing covenant children, the *Preface* then continues: "They be contained under the name of God's people.... Remission of sins in the blood of Christ Jesus doth appertain unto them by God's promise.... Paul...pronounceth the children begotten and born (either of the parents being faithful) to be clean and holy. First Corinthians 7.... "The Holy Ghost assure us that infants be of the number of God's people and that remission of sins doth also appertain to them in Christ.... Almighty God their Father." They are "His children bought with the blood of His dear Son."

The Belgic Confession, "This signifies to us that as water washes away the filth of the body when poured upon it, and is seen on the body of the baptized when sprinkled upon him, so does the blood of Christ by the power of the Holy Ghost internally sprinkle the soul...by the sprinkling of the precious blood of the Son.... 1

Corinthians 6:11; Titus 3:5; Hebrews 9:14; 1 John 1:7; Revelation 1:6."

Dr. G. de Bries (1608), "These two things we must observe in baptism. Namely, (1) the sign of water used as a seal, and (2) the body of those who have the truth of baptism.... The truth of baptism is also to be recognized in baptism.... That is the internal washing of souls in the blood of Christ...through the fellowship which we have with Him.... One should note...to whom the sign of baptism applies. Holy Scripture clearly teaches us that it applies to the entire household of God; to the whole body of His congregation; that is, to all of those who are His people, both small and large.... Little children...have the sproutings of faith.... One cannot include them among the unbelievers, until they come to their years or understanding....The little children are renewed by God's Spirit according to the measure and comprehension of their age. And this divine power, which is hidden within them, grows and gradually increases....they are redeemed, sanctified and regenerated from perdition — even though natural corruption still remains in them. For they possess such regeneration not through their own goodness, but through the sole goodness and mercy of God in Jesus Christ." G. de Briés: *The Radical Origin and Foundation of the Anabaptists*, ed. 1608, Bk. III. Ib. f. 290a.

Dr. Zacharias Ursinus, "'"Those are not to be excluded from baptism, to whom the benefit of remission of sins and of regeneration belongs. But this benefit belongs to the infants of the Church. For redemption from sin by the blood of Christ, and by the Holy Ghost the Author of faith, is promised to them no less than to the adults....We deny the proposition which denieth that infants do believe. For infants of believers regenerated by the Holy Spirit have an inclination to believe, or do believe by inclination. For faith is in infants — potentially, and by disposition.... Godly infants who are in the church, have...an inclination...to godliness — not by nature indeed, but by the grace of the covenant. "Infants have the Holy Ghost, and are regenerated by Him.... John was filled with the Holy Ghost, when as yet He was in the womb; and it was said to Jeremiah, 'Before thou camest out of the womb, I sanctified thee.' If infants have the Holy Ghost — then, doubtless, He worketh in them regeneration...unto salvation. As Peter saith, 'Who can forbid water — from them who have received the Holy Ghost as well as we?'" Z. Ursinus's Commentary on the Heidelberg Catechism, Q. 74 (cited in C. Coleburn's Scriptural, *Confessional and Historical References on the Regeneration of Children*, and their Status before the Lord and in the Church, Brisbane, 1991, p. 10.); and his *Christian Religion* Q. 74 (cited in Shedd's Dogmatic Theology (1894), Zondervan, Grand Rapids, 1969 ed., III pp. 443f).

Appendix 2

Dr. Zacharias Ursinus, "Covenant infants "are regenerated and belong to the people of God and to the body of Christ.... The gift of the Holy Spirit applies to the children of believers even before faith and conversion.... In general, it is from the covenant and the divine promise that one judges children to have been gifted with the Holy Spirit.... They are to be regarded as partakers of the Spirit of regeneration, by virtue of their birth in the Church and by power of the promises of God.... The actual reason why anyone should be baptized, is not faith and profession but regeneration...the gift of the Holy Spirit.... All believers are to be baptized; and only believers are to be baptized."

Dr. Casper Oliveanus, "Thus, our children are holy — by way of the Covenant of Grace.... See 1 Corinthians 7:14 and Ezra 9:2.... The promise of the Gospel has been made expressly to our children, Deuteronomy 30:6.... God consummated internally that which He promises externally. Titus 3:3-8...Everlasting life is sealed by the testimony of the Holy Spirit and imparted by the Holy Spirit." Casper Olevianus: *The Essence of the Covenant of Grace.* Copinga's translation, Groningen, 1739, pp. 497f.

The Second Helvetic Confession, "We condemn the Anabaptists, who deny that new-born infants of the faithful are to be baptized. For, according to evangelical teaching, of such is the Kingdom of God (Luke 18:16) — and they are written in the covenant of God (Acts 3:25) ... Why, then, should the sign of God's covenant not be given to them? Why should those who belong to God...and are in God's Church — not be initiated by holy baptism? We condemn the Anabaptists." 2nd Helv. Conf. chs. 11, 19-22, 30. "Damnamus Anabaptistas" (twice, in arts. 22 & 30). 83) Op. cit. p. 206. 84) *Creeds I,* p. 644.

Dr. Theodore Beza, "'The Anabaptists greatly err by opposing the baptism of infants.... Although they may not have faith with its effects such as those who are of age — they may, however, have the seed and germ of it; seeing that the Lord has sanctified them from the mother's womb (1 Corinthians 7:14) ... We presuppose in general that they are children of God — who are born of a believing father and mother, or when one of the two is a believer (Genesis 17:7)." Further, "as regards children born in the Church, one should presume the election of all of them, without limitation." Dr. Theodore Beza, *The Christian Faith* (1558.)

Italian Reformer Dr. Jerome Zanchius (Professor of Old Testament at Strassburg), "The precondition of receiving baptism, is that the baptizees have been gifted with the Spirit of faith...." Jerome Zanchius: *Theological*

Appendix 2

Works on External Worship IV c. 440. Cited in Kramer's op. cit. pp. 277ff.

Caspar vander Heyden, "Seed rests for a time in the earth, and takes root before one sees from its fruit that it has germinated.... The root of understanding and of reason has been poured into all children, as soon as they receive life.... God has planted a seed and a root of regeneration in the children of the covenant.... In time, the fruits of the Spirit germinate from it. For he who has been baptized with Christ in His death, also grows from Him, like a tender shoot on a vine...." Caspar vander Heyden, *Short and Clear Proofs of Holy Baptism*, (Moderator of the great Dutch Reformed Synods of Emden in 1571 and Dordrecht in 1574.)

Polyander, "We do, with the Scripture, pre-require faith and repentance in all that are to be baptized, at least according to the judgment of charity.... And that — also in infants that are within the covenant, in whom...we affirm that there is the seed and Spirit of faith and repentance." Polyander and Others: Synopsis of Purer Theology, 1581, Disp. 44c & 47 v. 9. Cited in H. Heppe's *Reformed Dogmatics*, Baker, 1950 rep., p. 609.

Francis Junius, "Junius also stated that "faith in its first action...is required.... For it is inseparable from the person covenanted or to be baptized.... It is an error to maintain absolutely that children cannot believe. For they have the beginning of possessing faith, because they possess the Spirit of faith (Spiritum fidei)...." Francis Junius' *Theological Theses on Paedobaptism*, page 139.

Dr. F. Nigel Lee, "At least half of the paedobaptistic rationale for infant baptism well rests on the presumption of regeneration in the babies concerned." F. Nigel Lee, section 5, *Baby Belief from Knox Till the Westminster Standards*.

Lucas Trelcatius Senior (1587) (Professor of Reformed Theology at Leyden), ""infants have the seed of faith" — 'fidem habent infantes in sementi.'..." the child of believing parents is sanctified, although not producing the fruits of conversion." Junius: op. cit. II c. 287, and his Nature and Grace, pp. 83ff. (as cited in Warfield's Two Stud. p. 203). cf. his *On Paedobaptism* 7 & 26.

Jeremiah Basting (trained by Beza, Ursinus and Olevianus, 1575.), "The sign and external ceremony can no way be denied those who are promised and given the things signified, such as forgiveness of sins and the Holy Spirit.... The immature little children are promised and given the forgiveness of sins and the Holy Spirit. How then can the element of water fairly be withheld from the young children?" J. Basting: Explanations of the [Heidelberg] Catechism of the Christian Religion

(1594), 2nd ed., comp. Rutgers's *Biblical References*, pp. 366ff.

William Bucanus (1609), "'It is not to be denied that the seed even of faith is poured into elect infants."R. Puppius's *Proof of Infant Baptism* (1611).

The Synod of Dordt, "As Calvinists, "our first position against the Lutherans who teach that baptism produces an active faith, is that tiny little children do not have an active faith...." Our second position, against the Anabaptists, is that the tiny little children are implanted with a seed of faith from which the later act of faith is born." In actual fact, however, "infants of believers have some seed of faith. At a more mature age, it goes forth to act. It accedes outwardly by human initiation, but inwardly by the Holy Spirit — with a greater effect." *Decrees of Dordt* I:17.

Such elect ones also include many babies. For Dordt insisted that "the children of believers are holy not by nature but by virtue of the Covenant of Grace in which they, together with the parents, are comprehended. Godly parents have no reason to doubt the election and salvation of those their children whom it pleases God to call out of this life in their infancy. 1 Corinthians 7:14; Genesis 17:7; Isaiah 59:21; Acts 2:39." In Vander *Waal's*, p. 53. Comp. too Gravemeijer: III:20:22 p. 139.

Dr. Festus Hommius, Stated Clerk of the Synod of Dordt (Regent of the Leyden State College, 1619.), "The children of believers "may not be reckoned among the positive unbelievers....because they do possess faith in its first actions, at the root and in the seed, and indeed through the internal operations of the Holy Spirit." F. Hommius: *Theological Disputations Against the Papists*, disp. 44, thes. 3, p. 269.

Andre Rivetus (French Reformed theologian, 1581) Professor at Leyden in 1620., "Covenant children have "the beginnings of possessing...the seed of faith.... For as the Kingdom of heaven belongs to them, so too does the Spirit of faith (Matthew 19:14) ..." A. Rivetus: *Disputes* 13, para. 13, p. 306; *Synopsis of Purer Theology*, III p. 305a, in Summa cont. tract.

Dr. William Ames, "Regeneration is a part of the promises, and applies to the children of the believers in a special way.... People are baptized because they are regarded as children of God, and not so that they should begin to become sons. Otherwise, there would be no reason not to baptize the children of unbelievers as well as children of believers." William Ames: *Bellarmine Unnerved*, II:1 p. 337.

Appendix 2

Dr. Voetius (Professor of Theology, Utrecht), "Covenant Infants, "are entitled to baptism: not because they are 'regarded' as members of the covenant, but because as a rule they actually already 'possess' the first grace. And for this reason, and this reason alone, it (the Formula) reads 'that our children...have been sanctified in Christ, and therefore ought to be baptized.'"

"In elect children belonging to the covenant, there is a first implantation of regeneration by the Holy Spirit. Thereby, the beginning and the seed of faith is implanted. From this, conversion and vital renewal must later take place at their own time. However, I reject (improbo) that regeneration takes place after baptism. For the opinion of our Reformed theologians are well-known. Baptism does not effect regeneration, but it is the sign of a regeneration which has already occurred. (Efficacia baptismi non in producenda regeneratione, sed in iam producta obsignata)...."From the seed (e semine)..., the actual dispositions and habits are sustained by the ingrafted operation of the Holy Spirit in His Own time.... Just like a seed, the abilities and possession of faith make their appearances by fresh acts of the Holy Spirit in their own time." All born in the covenant, who die before coming to an age of discretion, are believed to partake of heavenly salvation." Voetius, Dutch Reformed Baptismal Formula of 1581, 238), as cited in A. Kuyper Sr.'s *The Work of the Holy Spirit*, ET,

Eerdmans, Grand Rapids, 1941, p. 239, 300) G. Voetius: *Theological Disputations* (Biblical Preface IV pp. 254f). Cited in Kuyper's E Voto, III pp. 57ff. 240) Ib. II p. 417.

Dr. Jan Cloppenburgh (Amsterdam, Professor of Theology in Hardewyk, and Franeker), "Covenant children "possess the seed of faith within them....It not merely follows but also precedes baptism — and is accompanied by the fulfilments of the promises...." Jan Cloppenburgh: *The Gangrene of Anabaptist Theology*, II ch. 20 p. 245, cf. III ch. 28 p. 584ff.

Richard Sibbes, "Infants that die in their infancy...are within the covenant.... They have the seed of believing, the Spirit of God, in them.... If when they come to years, they answer not the Covenant of Grace and the answer of a good conscience..., all is frustrated ... we leave infants to the mercy of God." Richard Sibbes: *Works*, Banner of Truth, Edinburgh, 1983 ed., VI pp. 22f, & VII pp. 486ff.

Dr. Cornelius Burgess, ""The principal point handled in that work, is "that all elect infants...do ordinarily receive from Christ...the Spirit of regeneration as the...first principle of spiritual life." This they receive, "for their solemn initiation into Christ, and for their future actual renovation in God's good time – if they live to years of discretion." Cornelius Burgess: *The Regeneration of*

Appendix 2

Elect Infants professed by the Church of England, Curteyn, Oxford, 1629.

George Gillespie (Scottish Presbyterian Commissioner to the Westminster Assembly), "The sacrament is not a converting but a confirming and sealing ordinance..., to seal unto a man that interest in Christ and in the Covenant of Grace which he already hath. The sacraments do not give any grace, but do declare and show what God hath given. "Baptism is intended only for the redeemed of the Lord." Gillespie: *Aaron's Rod*, 1st ed., III ch. XII p. 489.

Stephen Marshall (Westminster Divine), ""Ever since God gathered a...select number out of the world to be His kingdom..., He would have the infants of all who are taken into covenant with Him to be accounted His — to belong to Him...and not to the devils.... "Being only passive in them all..., of this first grace is the sacrament of baptism properly a seal.... Who ever will deny that infants are capable of these things, as well as grown men – must deny that any infants dying in their infancy are saved by Christ." Stephen Marshall: *A Sermon on the Baptizing of Infants*, Coates, Bowtell, London, 1644, pp. 14, 25ff, 32, 26ff, 39, 41ff, 45ff & 51ff.

Dr. Edward Reynolds (Westminster Divine), "Nigel Lee says, "More than anybody else, it was probably Reynolds who drafted chapters 27 and 28 (of the Confession) on the subject of baptism." Reynolds says, "The promises and Word of grace, with the sacraments, are all but as so many sealed deeds to make over into all successions of the Church — so long as they contain legitimate children and observe the laws of their part required –an infallible claim and title....The nature of a sacrament is to be representative of a substance; the sign of a covenant; the seal of a purchase; the figure of a body; the witness of our faith; the earnest of our hope; the presence of things distant; the sight of things absent; the taste of things inconceivable; and the knowledge of things that are past knowledge." Edward Reynolds: *Meditations on the Holy Sacrament*, London, 1826 (1626?). Cited in Vincent's op. cit. pp. 18f & 30 n. 46.

Rev. Samuel Rutherford, "Who they are, who are to be baptized — it is presumed they give some professed consent to the call.... What ground is there to exclude sucking children? For...there is no Name under heaven by which men may be saved, but by the Name of Jesus...."Since Christ prayed for infants and blessed them — which is a praying for them — He must own them as 'blessed' in Christ in Whom all the nations of the earth are blessed.... It is false that the promise is made only to the aged... It is made to their children.... For the way of their believing — we leave it to the Lord." Samuel Rutherford, *The Covenant of Life Opened*, Anderson,

Edinburgh, 1655, I, chps. 13-14, pp. 72-91ff; cf. too his *Triumph of Faith* (in his Sermons VIII).315) Id., cited in Coleborn's op. cit. pp. 21ff, also republished by Puritan Publications.

Rev. John Wallis (Secretary of the Westminster Assembly), ""...we have no reason to doubt but many children very early, and even before their birth, may have the habits of grace infused into them — by which they are saved.... For as the habits of corruption, which we call Original Sin, by propagation — so may the habits of grace, by infusion, be inherent in the soul long before (for want of the use of reason) we are in capacity to act." John Wallis: *A Defence of Infant Baptism*, Oxford, 1657. Cited in Coleburn's op. cit., April 1991 ed., pp. 15ff.

John Calvin, "By these words, Christ...by a sacred bond...connects baptism with doctrine.... But as Christ enjoins them to teach before baptizing, and desires that none but believers shall be admitted to baptism — it would appear that baptism is not properly administered, unless when it is preceded by faith." John Calvin, *Commentary on Matthew* 28:19.

John Calvin, "Are we not, independent of baptism, cleansed by the blood of Christ and regenerated by the Spirit?" Indeed: "Let him (Heshusius) then accuse Paul of blasphemy — for saying that Christ is formed in us like the fetus in the womb. His well-known words to the Galatians are: 'My little children, for whom I again travail, as in birth — until Christ Jesus be formed in you.' Galatians 4:9...."

"God therefore calls those who were thus slain — 'His sons.' Just as if a husband should reproach his wife with depriving him of their common children.... Children are more precious than all goods.... A father is more grievously injured, if children are taken away.... God here pronounces... 'you have born them — unto Me.'"

"The Jews were naturally accursed, through being Adam's seed. But by supernatural and singular privilege, they were exempt and free from the curse — since circumcision was a testimony of the adoption by which God had consecrated them to Himself. Hence, they were holy.... As to their being impure, it could not...abolish God's covenant.... And so Paul says that the children of the faithful are holy — since baptism does not lose its efficacy, and the adoption of God remains fixed. 1 Corinthians 7:14." Calvin's <u>True Partaking of the Flesh and Blood of Christ in the Holy Supper</u>, in his *Tracts & Treat.* II pp. 497f. 306) Ib. pp. 534ff.

Dr. Thomas Manton, "Of those children, dying in infancy, I assert that they have...the seed of faith...in the covenant.... It must be so.... Socinians...count the faith of infants a thing so impossible, that they say it is a greater dotage than the dream of a man in a fever ... So those expressions of trusting God from the mother's womb. David speaks it of his own person, as a type of Christ. Psalm 22:9, 'Thou didst make me hope when I was upon my mother's breasts'.... Job saith, chapter 31:18, 'from my youth, he was brought up with me as with a father; and I have guided her, from my mother's womb' — meaning, he had a...disposition of pity put into him at his nativity. So also — why may not a principle of faith be put into us in the womb, if God will work it?" "What is the faith which children have? They have the seed of faith or some principle of grace conveyed into their souls by the hidden operation of the Spirit of God, which gives them an interest in Christ and so a right to His merit for their salvation...." Thomas Manton: *Complete Works*, Maranatha, Worthington Pa, rep. ed., n.d. (ca. 1975), XIV pp. 81-89 & 205.

David Dickson, "Truth's Victory Over Error, David Dickson asked: "Are elect infants, dying in infancy, regenerated and saved by Christ through the Spirit Who worketh when and where and how He pleaseth?" Echoing the Westminster Confession (10:3) itself, he answered, "Yes. Luke 18:15-16; Acts 2:38-39; John 3:3-5; 1 John 5:12." Dr. David Dickson, *Truth's Victory Over Error*.

David Dickson, "The precise time of begun regeneration is not always observed nor known either by the regenerate man himself or by beholders of his way." This "experience makes evident — in many who from their infancy are brought up in the exercises of true religion, in whose conversion no notable change can be observed." Dr. David Dickson, *Therapeutica Sacra*...Concerning Regeneration.

Dutch Calvinist Cornelius Poudroyen, "Believers' children "have the Holy Spirit and the redemption from sin — just as the adults do." "1 Corinthians 7:14 — 'Otherwise your children would be unclean; but now, they are holy.'" "...one cannot be holy, without the Holy Spirit.... Children have faith."

"The root and seed of faith, from which the Holy Spirit ignites and inflames their spiritual zeal when they increase in years.... They have the Spirit of Christ.... Wherever the Spirit of Christ is, there too is faith — whether an active faith, as in adults; or whether the root and origin of faith, as in small children."

Wendelin of Heidelberg (1656, German Reformed theologian), Christian System of Theology. Collation of Christian Doctrine from the Calvinists and the Lutherans, "The 'possessed faith' which we attribute to infants, we truly call — either 'the root' or 'the seed' of faith." M.F. Wendelin: *Christian System of Theology*, Cassel, 1656. Cited in Kuyper's *On the Sacraments* p. 142 (in his Dog. Dict. IV). Also, Wendelin's *Collation of Christian Doctrine from the Calvinists and the Lutherans*, Cassel, 1660, p. 352. See in Heppe's op. cit. pp. 624 & 714.

Herman Witsius, "Here certainly appears the extraordinary love of our God — in that as soon as we are born, and just as we come from our mother, He hath commanded us to be solemnly brought from her bosom as it were into His own arms, that He should bestow upon us in the very cradle the (baptismal) tokens of our dignity...."

"There can hardly be any doubt that the statement regarding the regeneration of the children before baptism, according to the judgment of love, is the accepted view of the Dutch Church. In her Baptismal Formula, this question is put to parents who offer their children in baptism: 'Do you acknowledge that they are sanctified in Christ, and should be baptized as members of His congregation?' "Now this strengthens the views of those who place the initial regeneration of elect covenant children before baptism. So, I acknowledge I submit to this."

"The children are regenerated, but the seed remains hidden for many years under the earth-clod. It is not choked by the thorns and thistles of youthful desires. Later, by addition of more grace, it finally surmounts the hindrances – and germinates and breaks forth more strongly and fortuitously.... God is not only free to impart the grace of regeneration to the elect children before they receive baptism. It should be believed that He, as a rule, also does this." Herman Witsius: *The Efficacy of Baptism in Infants*, in his *Holy Miscellanies* II exerc. 19 pp. 611-98 para. 32 (cited in Kramer's op. cit. pp. 337-38) Witsius: op. cit. para. 43, as cited in Kramer's op. cit. p. 339.

Thomas Watson, "Baptism...is a matriculation or visible admission of children into the congregation of Christ's flock...." To such as belong to the election, baptism is a 'seal of the righteousness of faith'...and a badge of adoption. Romans 4:11.... The infant seed of believers may as well lay a claim to the Covenant of Grace as their parents.... They cannot justly be denied baptism, which is its seal.... Does not their faith need strengthening, as well as others?" Thomas Watson, *Body of Divinity* (1670).

John Henry Heidegger (Swiss Reformed), "Regenerated and sanctified even in their mother's womb..., baptism is presently the sign of a regeneration already made and persevering right up to death." "However, that operation of the Holy Spirit is hidden.... For those who die in infancy, baptism is as surely the sign of regeneration and of ingrafting into Christ — as their body is surely sprinkled with water." J.H. Heidegger's *Body of Theology* (Zurich 1700) and his *Marrow of Christian Theology* XXV:50 & 53 & 55 (Zurich 1696). Cited in Heppe (op. cit. pp. 620 & 622 & 715) and in A. Kuyper (Sac. in Dict. Dog. IV p. 143).

Francis Turretin, "Covenant "children are just as much to be baptized as adults...the faith of covenant infants...consists of an initial action in them." That infant faith is "in root, not in fruit." It is characterized "by an internal action of the Spirit, not by an external demonstration in works." Francis Turretin: *Theological Elenctics* p. 427.

Wilhelmus A'Brakel, ""Whether dying before or after receiving baptism, all children of covenanters are to be regarded as saved — by virtue of God's covenant in which they were born.... Even the children are acknowledged to have been sanctified in Christ...." Wilhelmus A'Brakel, *Of the Christian's Reasonable Service*, 31:14 & 39:26.

Peter van Mastricht (Professor of Theology at Utrecht), "Children of the covenant should be baptized "because they partake of the benefits of the Covenant of Grace, of regeneration, and of the forgiveness of sin.... We are ordered in Holy Scripture to baptize as many as have received the Holy Spirit.... According to that Holy Scripture – Luke 1:15 & Jeremiah 1:5 — tiny children receive the Holy Spirit." Peter Van Mastricht: *Theoretical-Practical Theology*, Amsterdam, 1725, III p. 617. Cited in Kuyper's E Voto, III p. 58.

A.A. Hodge, "The children of all such persons (believing parents) are...presumptively heirs of the blessings of the Covenant of Grace. The divinely appointed and guaranteed presumption is — if the parents, then the children" too. "This presumption is rendered exceedingly probable, by the fundamental constitution of humanity as a self-propagative race....'" A.A. Hodge: *Evangelical Theology* (1890), Banner of Truth, Edinburgh, 1976 ed., pp. ii, 324-37.

Dr. William Cunningham, "The Reformers and the great body of Protestant divines, in putting forth the definition of the sacraments..., intended to embody the substance of what they believe Scripture to teach.... They commonly assume that the persons partaking in them, are rightly qualified for receiving and improving them.... Justification and regeneration by faith are not conveyed through the instrumentality of the sacraments.... On the contrary, they must already exist — before even baptism can be received lawfully or safely" Dr. William Cunningham *Historical Theology*, II, pp. 144 & 149.

B.B. Warfield, "All Protestants should easily agree that only Christ's children have a right to the ordinance of infant baptism.... We say that it (the Church) should receive as the children of Christ — all whom in the judgment of charity it may fairly recognize as such....All baptism is inevitably administered on the basis not of knowledge but of presumption....If we must baptize on presumption, the whole principle is yielded.... We must baptize all whom we may fairly presume to be Members of Christ's body.... "So soon, therefore, as it is fairly apprehended that we baptize on presumption and not on knowledge — it is inevitable that we shall baptize all those for whom we may, on any grounds, fairly cherish a good presumption that they belong to God's people.... This surely includes the infant children of believers." B.B. Warfield, *The Polemics of Infant Baptism*.

B.B. Warfield, "Among the Reformed alone ... (regarding the Invisible Church) of the people of God, membership...is mediated not by the external act of baptism but the internal regeneration of the Holy Spirit.... In the case of infants dying in infancy, birth within the bounds of the covenant is a sure sign, since the promise is 'unto us and our children.'" B.B. Warfield, *Studies in Theology* pp. 429ff & 447.

Herman Bavinck, "Men had this feeling that the regeneration of children took place before baptism.... God was not bound to means.... He operated thus with the children of believers who were removed by death before the years of discretion.... "They are to be regarded as elect and regenerate, until the opposite is apparent from their profession and behaviour.... All children born of believing parents are, according to the judgment of charity, to be regarded as born again — until the opposite in life and doctrine are clearly manifested. Thus Peter Martyr Vermigli, Alasco, Ursinus, Datheen, Alting, Voetius, Witsius, Mastricht...." Calvin says...that the children of believers are already holy even before baptism through a supranatural grace (Institutes IV:16:31); that the seed of faith and conversion hides within them through a secret operation of the Spirit (IV:16:20); that they partake of the grace of regeneration by virtue of the promise; and that baptism follows by way of sign.... Men had this feeling that the regeneration of children took place before baptism...." Herman Bavinck: *Reformed Dogmatics* I p. 29 & n. 1, and III pp. 266ff (as cited in Wielenga's op. cit. pp. 241ff).

Louis Berkhof, "From the start, there was general agreement in establishing the right of infant baptism — by an appeal to Scripture, and particularly to the scriptural doctrine of the covenant. Children of believers are covenant children, and are therefore entitled to the sacrament. According to some, it warrants the assumption that children of believing parents are regenerated — until the contrary appears in doctrine or life. At that latter point, the assumption would need to be revised." Louis Berkhof: *The History of Christian Doctrine*, Eerdmans, Grand Rapids, 1969, pp. 258ff.

In the neglect of understanding the doctrine of "presumptive regeneration," Charles Hodge said, "we have long felt and often expressed the conviction that this is one of the most serious evils in the present state of our churches." (Bushnell's discourses on Christian Nurture, *Biblical Repertory and Princeton Review* (1847), 19, Pages 52-521.)

Other Helpful Books by Puritan Publications

Infant Baptism God's Ordinance
by Michael Harrison (1640-1729)

Presumptive Regeneration, or, the Baptismal Regeneration of Elect Infants
by Cornelius Burgess (1589-1665)

The Doctrine and Practice of Infant Baptism
by John Brinsley (1600-1665)

Infant Baptism of Christ's Appointment
by Samuel Petto (1624–1711)

Covenant Holiness and Infant Baptism
by Thomas Blake (1597-1657)

A Discourse on Covenant Theology and Infant Baptism
by Cuthbert Sydenham (or Sidenham) (1622–1654)

The Rules of a Holy Life
by Nicholas Byfield (1579–1622)

The Covenant of Grace Opened
by Thomas Hooker (1586-1647)

The Way to Heaven
by John Philips (1585-1663)

www.ingramcontent.com/pod-product-compliance
Lightning Source LLC
LaVergne TN
LVHW041548070426
835507LV00011B/986